USING INFORMATION TECHNOLOGY

Marie Claire Williams

NVQ level **2**

Student Handbook

Heinemann Educational Publishers
Halley Court, Jordan Hill, Oxford OX2 8EJ
a division of Reed Educational & Professional Publishing Ltd

Heinemann is a registered trademark of Reed Educational & Professional Publishing Ltd

OXFORD   BLANTYRE   MELBOURNE   AUCKLAND
IBADAN   JOHANNESBURG   GABORONE
PORTSMOUTH NH (USA)   CHICAGO

First published 1997
2002 2001 2000 99 98 11 10 9 8 7 6 5 4 3 2

A catalogue record for this book is available from the British Library on request.

ISBN 0 435 452193

Typeset by TechType, Abingdon, Oxon

Printed and bound in Great Britain by
Biddles Ltd, Guildford and King's Lynn

Photo research by Jennifer Johnson
The author and publishers would like to thank the following
for permission to use photographs:

Trevor Hill
IBM UK Laboratories, Hursley
Ulrike Preuss, Format
Science Photo Library/Will & Deni McIntyre
SPL/Jerry Mason

Screen shots reproduced with permission from
Microsoft Corporation

Contents

The use of computers to carry out a very wide range of activities, for work, study and leisure, has become part of everyday life. It is no longer something that you *may* want to use if you are interested; rather like the motor car, it is an essential part of our lives. We are constantly told that anyone can use a computer, and to some extent this is true. However, as we become more and more dependent upon the technology this will not be enough.

What is needed are 'expert users'. These are people who know more than just which keys to press to make the computer work. These are people who know why. If you know why, then you are able to find out 'what if', and can therefore take full advantage of the potential of the computer in whatever area you are working. If you know why, you are more likely to be able to cope when the unexpected happens. Fault finding, solving problems and providing assistance to others depend upon knowing what to expect and what are the most likely causes of an unexpected result.

This book aims to give you the opportunity to take the first steps towards becoming an 'expert user'. It takes you through the basic knowledge you need and, by guiding you through a series of checklists and activities, helps you to find out about the computer equipment, the applications and the environment in which you are working. Using a number of case studies, you are given the opportunity to consider the roles and relationships that can exist within a working environment and how the technology can support and enhance the operation of the organisation.

With this knowledge and understanding, together with the specific applications skills that you will acquire as you use the packages, you will be well on the way to becoming an 'expert'. You should also have collected together a wide range of supporting evidence of this knowledge which can be used towards an NVQ Level 2 award in Using Information Technology.

What is an NVQ?

An NVQ (National Vocational Qualification) is a standard that has been introduced throughout the country specifically for work-based qualifications.

Assessment strategy

What is in the standards?

All NVQs consist of a number of *units*. A unit is a complete section of knowledge, e.g. how to use a computer and printer to produce documents to the satisfaction of your supervisor. Each unit is broken down into a number of *elements*, e.g. there are separate elements for entering the data, manipulating the data and printing the documents. Each element is described by a number of *performance criteria*. These spell out the things you have to be able to do and the skills and knowledge you need to demonstrate, e.g. all the required data is entered and this is done on time.

You are assessed against these standards and are required to demonstrate your competence for *all* the performance criteria and across a specified *range* (the scope and the variety) of activities.

A detailed description of each unit, element by element, starts on page 4.

Do you take an exam?

As this is a qualification to demonstrate your *skills* and *knowledge* for the workplace, you do **not** do exams but gather together evidence of your ability to do the work to an agreed set of standards. This evidence needs to be put together into a portfolio for assessment.

What form can the evidence take?

A number of different types of evidence can be used:

1   Observation of activities – your tutor/assessor/supervisor will need to watch you carrying out some of the tasks that you include in your portfolio of evidence.
2   End products – e.g. hard copy, disk files, etc.
3   Questions and answers (written and oral) – your tutor/assessor/supervisor may sit down and ask you questions or may give you a worksheet to complete.

4 Statements by yourself, supervisors and colleagues.
5 Projects and arranged assessments.
6 Previous certificates of competence, e.g. CLAIT or word processing certificates.

As this is a vocational qualification, the *primary* or main sources of evidence of competence wherever possible should be from (1) and (2) above, i.e. real work that you have done. Assessment may take place in a simulated environment, but only high-quality simulation which reflects the reality of a true workplace with its attendant constraints/pressures is acceptable.

Paper-based exercises may contribute towards evidence of competence but must *not* form the main body of evidence.

Presentation of your portfolio

Your portfolio will need to include the recording systems required by the awarding body. For each item of evidence this will need to show

- which *units, elements* and *performance criteria* it is evidence towards;
- who has assessed it; and
- when, where and under what conditions it was carried out.

You will need to compile an index and be able to cross-reference your documents.

As this NVQ is about working with new technology, you should be well equipped by the time you are completing your qualification to use many of the techniques of the software to enhance the presentation of your evidence.

The evidence you compile in your portfolio is assessed by an NVQ assessor and this assessment is confirmed by an internal verifier. An external verifier from the awarding body will also check a sample of the assessments.

Information about the structure of this NVQ

This NVQ is different from many others in two important ways. First, much of the evidence to demonstrate that you are competent comes from the product – that is, the work you produce using the computer. This means that it can be often possible to provide appropriate evidence in a simulated environment. Secondly, very few of the units are discrete – that is, they cannot be achieved in isolation from the other units. Whilst this means that much of the evidence for one unit is also evidence for other units, it also makes the recording, tracking and presentation of your completed portfolio more complex. However, this does mean that with a good index and clear cross-referencing of the contents of your portfolio you can cut down on the total volume of evidence you need to produce.

For this NVQ you are required to complete the five mandatory units and at least one of the three optional units. This book contains information about all the units. The optional unit you choose may, to some extent, be restricted by the computing facilities you have access to. If you are at work you are strongly advised to choose an option where it is easy for you to provide evidence – something you are already doing – not something completely different. You may find that you will need to negotiate additional training and computing opportunities outside your normal area of work to complete all the requirements of the qualification.

Whilst a large part of the qualification is concerned with the application of information technology and the demonstrated practical use of computers to carry out specified activities, it is not possible to achieve this without a good understanding and working knowledge of the complete installed computer system, its components, peripherals and facilities. You can't chose the *best* way to do something if you don't know the choices open to you. It is also essential to be able to demonstrate knowledge and awareness of the relevant legislation, especially with regard to data protection, computer misuse, software copyright, and health and safety.

Terminology

When you are studying for an NVQ, one of the first things you need to do is become familiar with the terminology that is used in the qualification. Included at the back of this book is a glossary of NVQ terminology. When a new term is first used it will be explained in the text. However, most people do not read textbooks from cover to cover, so if you come across a term you do not recognise or understand, have a look in the glossary before continuing.

Information technology (frequently referred to as IT) itself has an ever-growing set of terminology which you also need to learn. This will be treated in the same way – that is, when a new term is used it will be fully explained in the text and will also be included in the IT glossary at the back of the book. The terminology of computing is often confusing at first. It is, however, an important part of this qualification that you become familiar and at ease with the language used. You will be better able to cope with new aspects of the technology as you meet them and will also be able to communicate with 'experts' and will therefore be less likely to make wrong choices about what to use or buy.

A quick guide to understanding the standards

Some of the language used to set the standards in an NVQ needs to be turned into non-technical terms. This section is best used not by reading it from start to finish but as a reference that you will look at throughout the time you are working towards your qualification. Some of the words and phrases will only make sense to you when you start to do a particular task.

For each unit and element a brief description has been given for each of the performance criteria together, where appropriate, with some examples of what this might mean.

Unit 1: Enable use of information technology solution

This unit is about *operating* the equipment, using the appropriate storage media and using the appropriate software. This is demonstrated *throughout* the assessment period by using the equipment to carry out a range of activities correctly and in accordance with the requirements of the manufacturers, the organisation where you are using it and the legislation relevant to the working environment, such as health and safety and copyright law. Much of the evidence for this unit will be produced as you carry out tasks to meet the requirements of other units.

Element 1.1: Prepare use of information technology

a *Use of information technology solution to meet customer* requirements is accurately established*
Making sure that you know what the specific task is and that you need to use the computer to carry it out.

b *Equipment and materials are selected to meet customer requirements*
Demonstrating that you are using the correct equipment appropriate for the task in hand and the required materials, e.g. disks, letter-headed paper, etc.

c *Equipment is set up correctly in line with regulations*
Ensuring that you have the equipment set up properly, e.g. are you connected to the printer in the room you are working in? Does your VDU meet with health and safety regulations? Have you adjusted your chair to meet your needs? Is your workstation safely arranged?

d *Software is selected and accessed in accordance with regulations*
Using the right software for the task, e.g. should a particular task be done using a word processor or a spreadsheet? And ensuring

---

*Customer is the person for whom you are doing the work – it may be your supervisor, your tutor or even you if you work for yourself. It is the customer who sets the task.

that your access to the software meets with regulations, e.g. is the appropriate level of licence available?

e *Sources of data are correctly identified and when outside own authority verified*
Ensuring that you know where to get the necessary data to do the task, e.g. has all the data been given to you or do you need to ask for it? Can you find it yourself or does someone need to approve your use of it?

Element 1.2: Monitor use of information technology

The performance criteria for this element are best demonstrated through keeping records and log sheets of your use of the equipment, software and the working environment (furniture, cabling, etc.).

a *Working environment is monitored against regulations*
Checking that the equipment and workplace meet regulations, e.g. is the equipment correctly connected according to supplier's instructions?

b *Health and safety requirements are followed at all times*
Always *using* the equipment safely.

c *Appropriate records selected for updating are completed correctly and legibly*
Records of this monitoring, e.g. work sheets, log sheets, error logs, maintenance records, etc., should be kept up to date.

d *System integrity and security is preserved at all times*
Ensuring that you use the hardware, software and data correctly to reduce the likelihood of loss or damage and ensuring that unauthorised access does not take place. Your employer's records are valuable. If they are lost or damaged then the business might lose money. They are also confidential and must be protected from outsiders.

e *Materials selected are correctly used*
Using the disks and paper, etc., correctly, e.g. loading headed paper only when required, handling floppy disks appropriately to ensure they are not damaged.

f *Errors are correctly identified and dealt with in accordance with regulations*
Being aware when errors occur and ensuring they are dealt with correctly. This will include recording them and then either correcting them if that is within your role or reporting them in the appropriate way, e.g. moving an unsafe cable to a safer place or reporting it if this means rearranging the layout of the workstation. If the software package does not function as

expected you would need to report this; it is unlikely to be within your own role to attempt to put this right.

Element 1.3: Conclude use of information technology

This element will mainly be demonstrated through your correct use of the equipment, etc., and printouts of directories.

a *All necessary working data are saved conforming to organisation's standards and are in the correct location*
Saving your work as required, e.g. on the right disk and in the correct subdirectory.

b *Files are secured correctly and completely to a remote physical location*
Keeping security (backup) copies in a safe and different place, e.g. in another room, possibly in a fire safe.

c *Redundant files within own authority are deleted*
Deleting files you are responsible for that are no longer needed, e.g. exercises that are completed and marked.

d *Redundant files outside of own responsibility are dealt with in accordance with instructions*
Deleting files that you do not have direct responsibility for, e.g. deleting files that you have been told by your tutor or supervisor are no longer required.

e *Materials to be unloaded are identified and stored in designated location*
Changing and storing materials (paper, floppy disks, etc.) as required, e.g. taking letter-headed paper out of the printer when finished with and returning to where it is stored; clearly labelling floppy disks and removing them from drives and putting them away correctly when not in use.

f *Only those aspects of the system within authority are closed down*
Exiting correctly from the system, e.g. exiting a particular package when you have completed the required task, or exiting from your log-in area of a network. It can also mean *not* closing down the computer system completely because this may stop other people using it.

Unit 2: Produce documents using information technology solution

This unit is primarily about using the applications to produce and amend documents and will be mainly demonstrated through *using* the packages. Much of the evidence that you collect towards the optional units will also contribute to parts of this unit.

Element 2.1: Enter data to create and update files

a *Authority to access files and data is obtained as necessary*
Making sure that you are using data and files that you have been allowed to access, e.g. you have been told to take a copy of a file.

b *Files required to be updated are correctly identified and located*
Finding the files to be updated, e.g. accessing the file from the correct subdirectory.

c *Existing data to be updated are correctly identified, located and conform to requirements*
Updating the *specified* data, e.g. the right word is changed, the right paragraph is deleted, etc. If you're not sure about something you should check *exactly* what your supervisor wants changed.

d *Data are entered using appropriate device completely, correctly and to schedule*
Carrying out data input accurately and to an agreed timescale, e.g. if a spreadsheet is needed by your supervisor for a meeting, it is no use being 100 per cent accurate if it is not ready in time for the meeting.

e *Appropriate use is made of data checking facilities*
Checking your input, e.g. spellchecking *and* proofreading.

f *Files created or updated are saved conforming to agreed organisation's standards*
Saving files as required, e.g. using given filenames if required and in accordance with filenaming conventions if specified; remember, other people may need to be able to find these files.

Element 2.2: Produce required document by manipulating data

To cover the range required for the performance criteria for this unit you will need to work with numeric, text and graphical data.

a *Customer document requirements are accurately established, verified and checked*
Making sure you know what you are required to do, e.g. check with your supervisor if you are not exactly sure what is required.

b *Options for document layout and data formatting are identified and preferred solution agreed with customer*
Making sure that you know what layout is required, e.g. checking whether page 1 is to be numbered; you may wish to suggest an improved layout such as displaying the spreadsheet in landscape so that it all fits on one page.

c *Document handling facilities to input, select and combine stored data are correctly used to meet requirements*

Retrieving, sorting and merging documents correctly, e.g. mailmerge activity.

d *Facilities are used correctly and efficiently to structure the required document*
Using indexing, paragraph numbering and table of contents facilities correctly within the documents. You will need to know exactly what your software package can do and how to do it.

e *Facilities are used correctly and efficiently to layout and format the required document*
Using headers, footers, columns, indents and tabs correctly and creating the correct layout, e.g. putting a graphic in the right place.

f *Document is checked to be complete and error free*
Checking the completed document *before* submitting it as complete, ensuring that it is free from errors.

Element 2.3: Output specified document to destination

a *Appropriate destination is correctly selected*
Selecting the right printer or disk drive and directory.

b *The destination device is checked to ensure that it is able to receive output*
Making sure it is ready, e.g. printer is switched on, loaded with the correct paper or that the disk is in drive and not write protected.

c *Document is checked to be complete and correct prior to output*
Checking document *before* printing, e.g. spellcheck the document and proofread it on the screen, use the print preview to make sure the layout is appropriate.

d *Output parameters are identified and set up correctly to meet output requirements*
Outputting as specified, e.g. *only* printing a specified page or number of copies; printing a document in draft quality or suppressing the printing of the graphic when asked.

e *Document is output to correct destination*
Printing or saving to the right place, e.g. directing the printout of a confidential document to the printer that is not open to general access or saving the file to a floppy disk which is then removed and stored securely.

f *Output is checked to be complete and meets the customer's requirements*
Checking the document *after* printing, e.g. making sure all the pages have been printed, that the print quality is good and is what your supervisor wants.

Unit 3: Maintain the information technology solution

This unit is about looking after the equipment, the computer files and the documentation relating to the storage of data. It is mainly assessed through observation of you in the working environment and by the completion of records such as log sheets, fault reports, etc., *throughout* the assessment period.

Element 3.1: Maintain the equipment

  a *Equipment within own authority is cleaned as necessary*
  b *Equipment is cleaned according to regulations and with no effect on other users*
  d *Appropriate cleaning materials are identified and used in accordance with regulations*
     (a), (b) and (d) are about cleaning the equipment, e.g. cleaning the screens for which you are responsible with the correct materials taking into account safe use.

  c *Equipment is regularly monitored for wear and faults reported promptly*
     Checking for and recording any faults, e.g. damaged cables.

  e *Equipment diagnostic procedures are carried out regularly to regulations*
     For example, demonstrated by running a virus checker regularly.

  f *All diagnosed faults are reported promptly and with supporting evidence to the appropriate authority*
     Recording and reporting faults, e.g. immediately reporting any viruses; keeping a log for a printer that frequently jams to show to your technician or supplier.

Element 3.2: Maintain data file structures

This element is demonstrated through the records of disks and files and observation.

  a *Establish data file structures to meet customer requirements in accordance with regulations*
     Setting up directories and subdirectories to organise your files, e.g. your organisation may have a set of rules or guidelines on how to organise your data.

  b *File structure commands are identified and used correctly to create and maintain data file structures*
     Finding out how to use the operating system commands to set up and manage the directories using correct paths and directories.

  c *Correct locations are selected for the storage of data files*
     Selecting the correct directories in which to save files.

d *File operations within own authority are identified and correctly used*
Using the correct commands to move, copy, delete, name and
create files.

e *File structure security requirements are identified and implemented*
Carrying out backups and archiving as required.

f *Appropriate records maintained are correct, and complete*
Keeping the records of the backups and archives up to date and
printing out directory structures.

g *Media usage and available storage capacity are regularly checked to
meet present and anticipated storage requirements*
Checking space on disks, etc., to make sure there is room for
required files.

Element 3.3: Maintain media and documentation libraries

a *Media and documentation are selected for storage to meet regulations*
Identifying correctly software and backup data disks for secure
storage and the relevant documentation, such as backup logs and
software manuals.

b *Records of type and location of media and documents are maintained
correctly and clearly to meet regulations*
Keeping correct records of software and backup data storage so
that other people in the organisation can find them – also relates
to records of software and hardware manuals, e.g. booking-out/
booking-in records.

c *Media and documentation updates are correctly carried out as
appropriate*
Updating software and carrying out data backups as required and
also updating the records of these activities.

d *Media and documentation security and copyright requirements are
maintained at all times*
Ensuring that software, backups, manuals and records are kept
safely, e.g. file with backup records is kept in a place where it is
not likely to be damaged or accessed by unauthorised personnel.
A booking-out/booking-in system is kept to ensure that manuals
are not lost.

e *Environmental conditions are maintained to regulations*
Making sure that the storage environment is suitable for the
storage of magnetic and paper records particularly regarding
cleanliness, temperature, humidity and light conditions.

f *Redundant media are correctly located and disposed of in line with own
authority and regulations*
Disposing of out-of-date software and backups if this is within

your responsibility or under direction from the appropriate person, e.g. your supervisor might ask you to reformat a set of old backup disks.

Unit 4: Monitor the effectiveness of the information technology solution

This unit is about improving the way you and others use the computer system to carry out your tasks. It is concerned with how you go about organising your work and about working with your colleagues and supervisors.

Element 4.1: Contribute to improving the use of information technology

a *Facilities which aid effective use are accurately identified and recorded*
Finding out about facilities and features of the software and hardware which can assist in using the computer more effectively, e.g. setting up file manager or directory display to show the files in type of file order or creating a macro for an interactive memo format.

b *Potential improvements in use are identified and recorded*
Identifying improvements that these facilities could be used for and recording this.

c *Relevant proposals selected are communicated with supporting evidence to appropriate authority promptly*
Suggesting which improvements (changes) would be useful and how this could be achieved, e.g. writing a memo to your supervisor to suggest that a macro to run an interactive memo could be used by everyone in the department.

d *Resources obtained effectively meet requirements of own work*
Making sure that your computer and software are set up to meet your particular needs and making sure that you have the right type of disks. Also, making sure that you set and agree realistic deadlines to complete your work.

e *Materials are stored safely and securely and are located to provide ready access*
Storing your disks, paper, etc., in the right place, e.g. the department's supply of new disks and paper is kept locked in a stationery cupboard in the main office.

f *Resources are requested in accordance with organisational procedures*
Asking for the right paper, disks, software, hardware, etc., and following the organisation's rules, e.g. if you need to fill out a requisition form for a box of disks, do so.

Element 4.2: Improve own use of information technology

The world of IT is constantly changing. You will always need to keep your skills up to date. There will be upgrades to existing packages, new packages will be developed and you may need to learn how to use completely new applications. This unit is about being aware of this and how you can achieve this personal development.

a *Suggestions for improving own use are evaluated and implemented appropriately*
Identifying ways in which you could better use the technology and then carrying them out, e.g. you have been told by a colleague that you could extract the data held in the database to produce standard letters rather than creating a mailing list in the word processor – your colleague has agreed to show you how to do this.

b *Appropriate reference materials are selected and used for improving own use*
Using handouts, online help, manuals, books, etc., to find out how to use the hardware and software.

c *Development needs are identified and agreed with an appropriate authority*
Making sure that you have regular reviews of your training needs, e.g. whilst on the course you meet with your tutor to discuss these – in the workplace you may have regular (6-monthly) reviews with your line manager.

d *Development plan devised is agreed with appropriate authority to meet identified needs*
Making sure that a training plan is drawn up during the review process and that your supervisor agrees with it, e.g. you might suggest a training course you need to attend or a book you need to buy so that you can acquire the identified skills and knowledge.

e *Development undertaken is in line with agreed plan and recorded*
Carrying out the agreed plan and making sure that this is recorded in your personal file.

Element 4.3: Contribute to effective use of information technology

NOTE: This element **must** be assessed in the workplace.

a *Tasks are identified and prioritised according to organisational procedures*
Identifying what work you have to do and what are the priorities, i.e. distinguishing between routine, unexpected and urgent tasks.

b *Appropriate planning aids are used to schedule work*
Organising your workload with the assistance of planning aids,
e.g. keeping a diary, schedule, task log – these may be both
electronic and paper-based.

c *Where priorities change, work schedules are adapted accordingly*
Rescheduling tasks to respond to events that change priorities and
recording this log of activities.

d *Anticipated difficulties in meeting deadlines are promptly reported to
the appropriate authority*
Alerting supervisor, etc., of possible delays, e.g. there are times
when it is not possible to complete a task by the deadline set; if
this happens you must talk to your supervisor and suggest a
solution.

e *Assistance is sought, where necessary, to meet specific demands and
deadlines*
Asking for help or support where necessary so that a task can be
completed on time, e.g. sometimes the deadline cannot be moved
but it may be possible for part of the work to be completed by
someone else – a colleague who does not have any critical
deadlines at the time may be willing to give you a hand to
complete an urgent job, particularly if he or she knows that you
will return the favour.

f *Wastage of resources is minimised*
Using resources such as paper and time thoughtfully, e.g. only
printing *after* spellchecking and proofreading on the screen. Time
is a very important resource – you shouldn't waste it.

g *Work practice is in accordance with organisation's standards*
Ensuring that the quality of the work produced is to a satisfactory
standard, e.g. word processed document is accurate and meets
the organisation's requirements on presentation so that it is
suitable for distribution.

Element 4.4: Establish and maintain working relationships with other colleagues

No one works in isolation; you must be able to get on with your
colleagues and work productively with them.

NOTE: This element **must** be assessed in the workplace.

a *Opportunities are taken to discuss work-related matters with relevant
colleagues*
Discussing work with your line manager, immediate colleagues
and other colleagues, e.g. checking what is wanted; someone you
work with may know the answer to an immediate problem or you
may be able to help him or her.

b *Essential information is passed to all appropriate colleagues promptly and correctly*
Passing on information without delay or error, e.g. taking accurate messages and passing them on – an urgent message from yesterday is probably too late and is of little use if you didn't write down the telephone number correctly.

c *Effective working relationships are maintained with individuals and teams*
Working co-operatively with others, e.g. making sure that you do not 'let down' your colleagues by not completing your part of an activity; providing assistance to complete an urgent task if your workload is light and less urgent.

d *Commitments to others are met within agreed timescales*
Ensuring that tasks for other people are done as agreed, e.g. you might need to delay going to lunch by 10 minutes so that you can print out a 'good' copy of an urgent letter for your supervisor.

e *Changes in agreed timescales are agreed with appropriate authority*
Making sure that if you need to change the agreed completion time for a task that your supervisor has agreed to this, e.g. although you had agreed to get all the routine data input completed a day early if possible, you have been given an urgent task which means that this will not now be possible – this shouldn't be a problem but make sure your supervisor knows.

f *Methods of communication and support used are suited to the needs of other colleagues*
Using best methods of communication, e.g. writing out details of a message if you are not able to speak to the person.

Unit 5: Monitor and maintain a healthy, safe and secure working environment

For this unit you will need to demonstrate your knowledge of relevant legislation and good working practices within a working environment and particularly in relation to a technology-rich environment.

Element 5.1: Monitor and maintain health and safety within the working environment

This element is concerned with knowing about, recording and reporting emergencies, accidents and faults.

a *Hazards are corrected if within own authority*
Correcting situations or events which present some form of health and safety hazard, e.g. repositioning your workstation so that it does not obstruct a passageway.

b *Hazards outside own authority are promptly and accurately reported to the appropriate authority*
Reporting to the correct person situations or events which present some form of health and safety hazard but for which you do not have authority to act yourself, e.g. changing the routing of cables.

c *Actions taken in dealing with emergencies conform to regulations*
Knowing the correct responses for emergencies including illness, accidents, fire and evacuation.

d *Emergencies are reported promptly and recorded correctly, completely and legibly in accordance with regulations*
Knowing the correct procedures for the reporting and recording of accidents and emergencies.

e *Working environments which do not conform to regulations are promptly and correctly reported to the appropriate authority*
Reporting to the appropriate person aspects of the working environment which do not conform to regulations, e.g. monitors that do not conform to EU directives.

f *Working environment is organised to minimise risk to self and others*
Organising your working environment to minimise risk to yourself and others, e.g. adjusting the height of your computer chair or adjusting the brightness and contrast on your monitor; not leaving cleansing fluid bottles open where they can be knocked over nor piles of papers where your colleagues can trip over them.

Element 5.2: Monitor and maintain the security of the working environment

This is about following the security procedures of the organisation regarding access to the working environment and the computer systems. Security is very important for anyone working with computers. If an unauthorised person gains access to an organisation's computer system he or she may be able to do untold damage or steal valuable information.

a *Organisational security procedures are carried out correctly*
Following the procedures of the organisation, e.g. not telling anyone what your password is, changing your password on a regular basis, not leaving your computer area open; keeping your security pass safe and not allowing anyone else to use it.

b *Potential breaches of security procedures are identified and reported*
Alerting your supervisor to any potential security risks, e.g. access to the computer system which is not protected; an unlocked door to a computer room where the door should be locked when unoccupied.

c *Identified security risks are corrected and reported promptly to the appropriate authority*
Correcting a security risk and alerting your supervisor of this, e.g. changing a password which is no longer secure because you have misplaced the piece of paper with the details (a very good reason for *not* writing down your password) and letting the relevant person in authority know that this has happened.

d *Breaches of security procedures are dealt with in accordance with organisational procedures*
Reporting a breach of security, e.g. the loss of a security pass.

Element 5.3: Monitor and maintain data security in the working environment

This element is concerned with data protection legislation and how it relates to the organisation you work in. It covers legislation regarding the misuse of computers, including copyright, fraud and theft.

a *Legislation applicable to data security in the working environment is identified and implemented*
Knowing the relevant aspects of the data protection legislation and ensuring that you are working within them.

b *Potential breaches of legislative procedures are identified and reported*
Being aware of aspects of your work which have special requirements in law, e.g. the need to shred unrequired printouts of personal data.

c *Breaches of legislative procedures are dealt with in accordance with organisational procedures*
Reporting breaches of the legislation and following the agreed procedures.

The final three units are optional. You need cover only one. You are strongly advised to choose a unit that fits in easily with the work you do or training that is readily available to you. If you are not at work, your tutor will advise you about your choice of option.

Unit 6: Produce numerical models using information technology solution

This element is primarily about using the applications to produce and amend worksheets and models and will mainly be assessed through the use of spreadsheets, including the production of graphs.

Element 6.1: Enter numerical data to create and update files

a *Authority to access files and data is obtained as necessary*
Making sure that you are using data and files you have been

allowed access to, e.g. you have been told to work with a particular file.

b *Files and data required are correctly identified and located*
Finding the files to be updated, e.g. working on the correct disk and subdirectory.

c *Numerical data to be updated are correctly identified, located and conform to requirements*
Updating the *specified* numeric data, e.g. the right number is changed, the right number is deleted, etc.

d *Numerical data are entered completely using appropriate input device correctly and to schedule*
Carrying out data input accurately and to an agreed timescale – this may be amending an existing file or creating a new one.

e *Appropriate use is made of data checking facilities*
Checking your input, e.g. the input results in the anticipated answers, using the print preview to make sure that it is presented in the best way – you might want to change from portrait to landscape so that all the columns are on one sheet.

f *Files saved conform to agreed organisation's standards*
Saving files in accordance with the organisation's standards, e.g. using given filenames if required.

Element 6.2: Produce required model by manipulating data

a *Customer numerical model requirements are accurately established, verified and checked*
Making sure you know what you are required to do, e.g. what the calculations are.

b *Options for model format and layout are identified and preferred solution agreed with customer*
Making sure that you know what layout is required, e.g. checking whether landscape layout is required or what column headings are needed – you may be able to suggest the preferred layout particularly if your customer is not an IT specialist.

c *Data handling facilities to input, select and combine stored data are correctly used to meet requirements*
Retrieving and sorting the data correctly.

d *Cell formatting facilities are used correctly and efficiently to structure the required model*
Using data format facilities correctly, e.g. two decimal places, right justified text, etc.

e *Cell range operations are used correctly and efficiently to meet the required model*

Using move, copy, delete, and absolute and relative cell references correctly and creating the correct layout.

f *Model is checked to be complete and error free*
Checking the completed document *before* submitting it.

Element 6.3: Produce graphical representation from numerical information

a *Appropriate graphical representation is selected to meet requirements*
Using the correct kind of graph, e.g. pie chart, line graph or bar chart which best displays the data.

b *Graphical representation parameters are selected and used correctly to meet requirements*
Using the right axes and scales and the desired orientation – a bar chart could be vertical or horizontal.

c *Graphical representation is annotated correctly to meet requirements*
Using the correct labels, legends and titles – without these the chart does not mean anything.

d *Numerical information to be represented is correctly selected and used*
Selecting the correct numerical data – the chart might *look* good but the data may not be valid.

Element 6.4: Output specified model to destination

a *Appropriate destination is correctly selected*
Selecting the right printer or disk drive and directory.

b *The destination device is checked to ensure that it is able to receive output*
Making sure it is ready, e.g. that the printer is switched on or that the disk is in the drive and is not write protected.

c *Model is verified and checked to be complete and correct prior to output*
Checking the spreadsheet model *before* printing it – using the print preview to see how it fits on the page, making sure all the required formulae are included.

d *Output parameters are identified and set up correctly to meet output requirements*
Outputting the model as specified, e.g. printing *only* a specified page or number of copies.

e *Model is sent to correct destination*
Printing or saving to the right place, e.g. directing the printout of a confidential document to the printer that is not open to general access or saving the file to a floppy disk which is then removed and stored securely.

f *Output is checked to be complete and meets the customer's requirements*

Checking the model *after* printing, e.g. making sure that all the pages have been printed, that the print quality is good and is what your supervisor wants.

Unit 7: Produce graphical images using information technology solution

This unit is primarily about using applications to work with graphical images and is mainly assessed through the production and manipulation of appropriate images. You will need to work with both vector and bitmap images which may be retrieved from clip art, images that you have scanned in and ones that you have drawn yourself.

Element 7.1: Enter data to create and update images

a *Authority to access files and images is obtained as necessary*
Making sure that you are using data and files that you have been allowed to access, e.g. making sure that the use of any images does not contravene copyright.

b *Sources of files and images required are correctly identified and located*
Finding the files to be updated, e.g. working on the correct disk and subdirectory.

c *Images are entered completely using appropriate input device correctly and to schedule*
Creating and editing images accurately using the correct input devices and to an agreed timescale, e.g. appropriate and accurate use of scanner, mouse and keyboard.

d *Files saved conform to agreed organisation's standards*
Saving files in accordance with the organisation's standards, e.g. using given filenames if required.

Element 7.2: Produce required graphical image by manipulating data

a *Customer graphical image requirements are accurately established, verified and checked*
Making sure you know what you are required to do, e.g. what images are required and for what purpose.

b *Options for graphical image are identified and preferred solution agreed with customer*
Identifying the different ways and sources for such images and agreeing which will be the most appropriate on grounds of time, quality, etc.

c *Facilities to enter, select and combine stored images are correctly used to meet requirements*

Working with previously stored images including combining them with other images.

d *Facilities are selected and used correctly to manipulate image*
Creating and manipulating images as required in terms of size, location, orientation, rotation and inversion.

e *Facilities to create additional elements are used correctly to meet requirements*
Adding elements of lines, shapes and text to existing images as required.

f *Facilities to alter attributes are used correctly to meet requirements*
Changing the colour, shade, patterns, size and shape of images as required.

g *Graphical image is checked to be complete and to customer requirements*
Ensuring that the final image is complete and that it is what is required.

Element 7.3: Output specified image to destination

a *Appropriate destination is correctly selected*
Selecting the right printer or disk drive and directory.

b *The destination device is checked to ensure that it is able to receive output*
Making sure it is ready, e.g. that the printer is switched on or that the disk is in the drive and is not write protected.

c *Image is verified and checked to be complete and correct prior to output*
Checking that the image is ready for use *before* printing it, e.g. using the print preview to see how it fits on the page.

d *Output parameters are identified and set up correctly to meet customer requirements*
Outputting the image as specified, e.g. printing *only* a specified page or number of copies or printing in colour/greyscale.

e *Image is sent to correct destination*
Printing or saving to the right place, e.g. making sure that you have sent the printout to the colour printer or the high-quality laser.

f *Output is checked to be complete and meets the customer's requirements*
Checking the image *after* printing, e.g. making sure that all the pages have been printed, that the print quality is good and is what your supervisor wants.

Unit 8: Communicate electronically using information technology solution

This unit is about electronic communications such as fax and e-mail and about working with databases, both local (such as in-house files) and remote (such as on the Internet).

Element 8.1: Transmit messages using information technology

a *Appropriate facilities for transmitting messages are selected*
Deciding whether to use fax, electronic mail or a bulletin board for a particular task.

b *Messages to be transmitted are checked for completeness and accuracy prior to transmission*
Making sure the message is complete *before* it is sent.

c *Appropriate transmission parameters are correctly entered*
Entering the correct e-mail address or fax number and number of copies.

d *Messages are transmitted correctly, completely and to regulations*
Ensuring that the message has been sent without any errors and following the guidelines and procedures of the organisation, e.g. using required fax transmission sheet, correcting errors such as part of the message not reaching its destination.

Element 8.2: Receive messages using information technology

a *Appropriate facilities for receiving messages are correctly selected and made ready*
Making sure that fax and electronic mail facilities are available and working and able to *receive* messages, e.g. fax/telephone is switched to receive faxes.

b *Appropriate location is regularly checked for messages*
Checking the fax machine and your mailbox and appropriate bulletin boards regularly for incoming messages.

c *Messages received are checked for completeness and accuracy*
Checking that received messages are complete, e.g. checking expected number of pages and contacting sender if anything is incomplete or unclear.

d *Messages received in error are referred to appropriate authority*
Making sure that mail that is not for you is forwarded as appropriate.

e *Messages are correctly processed to regulations*
Making sure that you are using the equipment and facilities safely and legally, e.g. passwords on mailboxes are not disclosed, fax machines are used following manufacturers' instructions.

Element 8.3: Access stored information system

a *Specified stored information system is accessed and checked to be available*
Using a range of data storage systems including e-mail and databases – both local and remote, e.g. data from the Internet and in-house including CD-ROMs.

b *Customer queries are formatted correctly to meet requirements*
Using correct query commands to extract the required information from a database.

c *Stored information system is correctly accessed in accordance with regulations*
Accessing databases that you have been authorised to use, and using them in line with the requirements of the Data Protection Act, e.g. making sure you are aware of the copyright status of data that you have accessed from the Internet, not disclosing personal data extracted from your organisation's files.

d *Information retrieved is verified to be timely, correct and meets customer requirements*
Making sure that the information retrieved is what is asked for and is on time, e.g. producing the required set of data with the right layout by the deadline.

Unit mapping grid

Element	Chap. 1	Chap. 2	Chap. 3	Chap. 4	Chap. 5	Chap. 6	Chap. 7	Chap. 8	Chap. 9
1.1		●	●		●	●		●	
1.2	●		●	●				●	●
1.3	●		●	●	●			●	
2.1	●	●		●	●	●			
2.2		●	●		●	●			
2.3		●	●	●		●			
3.1	●		●						●
3.2	●			●	●			●	
3.3	●		●	●	●			●	●
4.1	●	●					●		●
4.2	●						●		
4.3	●					●			
4.4	●							●	
5.1			●						●
5.2	●					●		●	
5.3					●			●	
6.1	●	●		●	●	●			
6.2		●			●	●			
6.3		●				●			
6.4		●	●		●				
7.1	●	●		●		●			
7.2		●				●			
7.3		●	●	●					
8.1						●			
8.2						●			
8.3						●			

NVQs are about the workplace. It is therefore necessary that you know about how organisations may be structured and how these structures can affect the different aspects of working relationships.

Organisational structure

Organisational structure defines the lines of authority and reporting. It defines where particular activities take place and how control is exercised. For most of us, the structure of the organisation we work for is often not apparent. We carry out the tasks we are required to do and often are not aware of the wider functioning of the whole.

However, when you are using data that is on a computer system, it is frequently data that is available across the whole organisation. The data that you input into the database or the form that you create is often going to be used by both the people you work with on a day-to-day basis and others whom you do not know and quite often are unaware of. It is therefore essential for you to know at least a little about the way your organisation is structured.

Most organisations have a written document showing their structure. This is usually drawn as a chart. In a large organisation this may consist of a general organisation chart detailing the different departments or sections and how they work together and separate charts to show the staffing structure (line management) in each department. For smaller organisations there may be just one chart that shows both the departmental and staffing details.

CASE STUDY: Avits Ltd

Alan and Vayo Tomas jointly own a company which makes and sells 3D Wingdings. Alan heads the design team and looks after the production side while Vayo oversees the sales, finance and general administration. The structure of the company is shown in the charts in Figures 1.1 and 1.2.

Using the information from the organisation chart and for the four departments, identify the line manager of the following staff:

1 The goods in/out clerk at the factory.
2 The payroll clerk in the Finance Department.
3 The sales supervisor in the Sales Department.

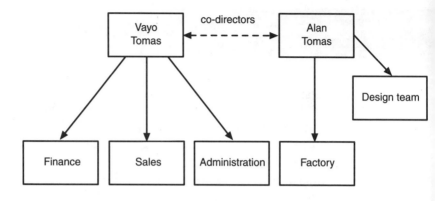

Figure 1.1 Avits Ltd: organisation chart

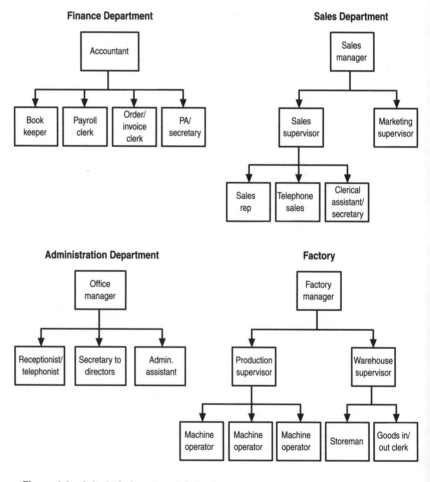

Figure 1.2 Avits Ltd: departmental structure

4 The accountant.

5 The secretary to the directors.

Confirm your answers with your tutor.

What is the structure for the organisation where you work or are gaining your work experience? Ask you supervisor for a copy of the organisation chart if there is one. If you are in a small organisation which has not created one, find out what the structure is and draw one of your own. You may wish to check with your supervisor to make sure that you have understood the organisation correctly – he or she may even want to use your chart when you have completed it. Place a copy of this in your evidence portfolio.

Line management and colleagues

Organisational structure is important – it lets you know who is in charge of what and who has authority over what. It helps to describe what activities people are responsible for and to whom they are accountable (answerable). Some organisations will be hierarchical, with many tiers or layers of structure, whilst others will have what is known as a 'flat' structure and will tend to be less formal. The type of structure of your organisation will to some extent dictate how you interact with your colleagues.

Your particular areas of responsibility and accountability will usually be clearly described in your job description. This document enables you to see what is 'in your own authority' and who your line manager is. The organisational structure enables you to see your role in the wider context of the organisation and will help you identify your relationships with people not only in your immediate area of work but also across the whole organisation.

In many jobs, although you will have your own specific areas of responsibility, you will also be part of a team. You need to be able to work with and support the other members of the team just as they need to be able to work with and support you.

Do you have a job description or, if you are on work placement, a list of activities you will be expected to do? Place a copy in your evidence folder as this is useful as supplementary evidence.

What skills do you need for working as part of a team?

CASE STUDY: Avits Ltd

Jason is the receptionist/telephonist at Avits Ltd. The job is located in the Administration Department and the job holder is responsible to the office manager.

A number of different activities are identified in the job description, including the following:

- Staffing the switchboard – this means that the job holder is usually the first point of contact for any callers to the organisation.
- Greeting visitors to the organisation – the job holder is located in the main reception area of the building.
- Sorting and distributing the incoming mail to all departments.
- Stamping, or franking, and sending out the outgoing mail.
- Word processing of some general correspondence – this is usually to provide support to any of the administrative and secretarial staff in the organisation when their workload is high.

a Which of these tasks do not affect anyone else's ability to do his or her job (if any)?

b Which of these tasks may *directly* affect someone else's ability to do his or her job?

c Which of these activities may *indirectly* affect someone else's ability to do his or her job?

d What personal attributes and skills do you think someone would need to do this job well?

Now think about your work. Can you identify those activities in your job which you would list under (a), (b) and (c)?

Working with colleagues

In almost every type of job, you need to work with others. To do this successfully, it is important to consider how you communicate with all sorts of people. The way you discuss a particular task or problem will be different when you are talking to your line manager, to a colleague in your section with whom you often have lunch, to others in the department with whom you are less likely to socialise, and to the person you are doing the work for (the customer).

The type of organisation you work for will have an influence upon the way you communicate and particularly the degree of formality that is expected. In an organisation with a hierarchial structure, communication systems will tend to be formal, with a greater emphasis on structured written communications such as forms, memos, e-mails and letters. In an organisation with a flatter structure many communications will be much less formal and, whilst there will still be a need for some records to be kept, there is often a greater use of verbal methods such as telephone and face-to-face conversation. The actual language used will also reflect the degree of formality in the organisation – the tone and structure of communication will be different.

However, whatever the organisation's structure, you will usually need to adjust your style for a range of types of communication. Each of the following will require a different approach:

- seeking advice
- clarifying requirements
- sending notification of completion
- alerting people to delays or problems
- requesting agreement to proposals
- asking for assistance.

 CASE STUDY: Avits Ltd

You work as the administration assistant in the Administration Department. The sales manager wishes to introduce a new logging system to record all the telephone sales. You have been asked to draw up the logging sheet and to circulate this to the staff in the Sales Department by tomorrow.

1   In order to get this completed in time you will need to ask your colleague, the secretary to the directors, Jan Watts, to help with the weekly filing so that you can complete this task in time. As Jan is not in the office until lunchtime, write a brief note asking for this assistance.
2   Write a draft memo to be sent to all the staff in the Sales Department informing them of the new system and asking for their comments on the proposed form. Also draft a memo with similar information to be sent to the two directors of the company.
3   Send a memo to the sales manager, Peter Secunda, alerting him to the possibility of the system being delayed if staff in his department are unable to respond to your request for comments quickly. Include in the memo a request to confirm the contents of the logging sheet.

Discuss with your tutor the differences in tone and structure that are appropriate in these communications.

Handling disagreements and conflicts

Wherever you are, but particularly in your work, there will be times when you have to deal with or work for someone you would not have chosen as a friend. However, you do need to be able to carry out your duties and get along. What you need is a strategy to be able to complete your work without upset to you or your colleagues. It is important to make sure that you take into account the implications of how you react and respond to disagreements and conflicts without allowing yourself to be taken advantage of.

You should consider ways of establishing constructive working relationships. You should make sure that you are aware of the 'politics' of the office, taking account of pressures that others might be under and assisting, whilst ensuring that your own workload does not suffer.

 CASE STUDY: Scorpion Business Solutions

Lauren works in the Sales Department of a computer company providing administrative support.

Below is a list of difficult situations, some with a colleague, some with a manager and others with a 'customer' (*remember* – it is likely that many of the tasks you do are for other people).

1 Lauren has word processed a document for a colleague because there was a tight deadline to meet. The task has been completed in time and has been given to the colleague with the printouts ready for mailing. This colleague has now come back and complained that page 14 of the 20-page document is missing.

2   Lauren has been asked to look up details in a customer file by the manager but the name of the customer has been misspelled in the request. Lauren has sent a note to say that there is no such customer on the computer system and the manager has said that she should have tried several spellings to find it.

3   Lauren has been asked to create a document with the company logo on the top. The requirement is that it must not go over on to a second page and that the size of the logo should therefore be reduced so that it all fits. Lauren has explained that the quality of the resulting logo in the document is poor because of the resolution of the printer but has been told that this is not acceptable.

4   At 4.30 in the afternoon Lauren has been given a complex spreadsheet to create. It is needed by 'the end of the day' but she has noticed that the date on the request is the day before yesterday.

5   It is Friday afternoon and Lauren's manager has already left for the weekend. A customer telephones with a complaint and insists quite rudely that he has been overcharged due to incompetence and wants a commitment to resolve the problem now.

In each situation, should Lauren:

a   bite her tongue and 'scream' about it later in private;
b   discuss the problem calmly but make it clear that she believes she is right;
c   tell the person concerned he or she does not make sense and can see Lauren's manager if he or she has a problem; or
d   complete the task grudgingly and complain later?

You might find it useful to discuss your answers with your colleagues in the workplace or your manager or supervisor.

Organisation standards

Every organisation has rules about the way it operates. These rules are not just the ones that are written down in your contract of employment or your college student agreement, but they include the rules and conventions that enable the organisation and the people within it to function effectively, efficiently and happily. These can cover everything from the size and font of business communications to the type of dress code expected. So that an organisation can function as one body, it is necessary to define standards to which all staff will work. You may think 15 point Gothic is the ideal typeface for correspondence, but if your organisation prefers 12 point Times, 12 point Times is what it should get. There will be some areas where there is room for you to use your own initiative, others where you do what your boss demands. Part of being at work is learning to identify those situations when you can use your own judgement, those when you need to persuade a more senior colleague of the value of implementing a new idea – and those when you accept the status quo unquestioningly.

Information handling

Almost everything you do in your work will involve working with some form of information. You may be preparing documents, entering data into the computer, answering the telephone, organising a meeting and so on. One of the most important aspects of all of this is that you ensure as far as you can that the information is *correct* and *timely*.

The chapter on working with data looks particularly at ensuring the correctness of the data as it is processed in a computer system. All the activities that take place away from the computer also need to be considered.

In a task such as taking messages, there are a number of steps you can take to make sure that you have done everything necessary to pass on the information.

 CASE STUDY: Scorpion Business Solutions

Lauren has received the following messages. How should each one be handled to make sure that it is accurate and reaches its destination, taking into account the nature of the message?

1 There is a telephone message for the manager's secretary giving details of the postponement of a meeting this afternoon.
2 A note has been left by a customer for a colleague about a change to an order.
3 There is a fax from a salesperson about a competitor's product promotion starting next week.
4 A phone call has been received for the payroll officer giving bank details for a new member of staff.
5 Just as Lauren's manager was going out of the door, he asked Lauren to phone his business partner to remind her about the meeting at 8.30 tomorrow morning, but there is no reply.

Discuss your answers with your tutor.

Confidential information

Some of the information you will be working with will probably be confidential. Almost all organisations have some data that should not be freely available. There will be many different reasons why information is considered to be confidential. Some aspects of confidentiality of data are covered by legislation. Refer to the section on the Data Protection Act; remember, almost all *personal* data held in electronic form is covered by this legislation.

There are, however, many other reasons for not giving unrestricted access to information. Most organisations will store, in one form or another, large quantities of information about their own business. This will probably include details regarding financial viability, share of the market in terms of sales and customers, products and services and research and development plans.

In some organisations a great deal of effort is put into maintaining the confidentiality of information whilst it is in the computer system, with elaborate password systems and controls on access to the data. However, once the information is printed on paper the level of security often drops.

Do you have:

- secure printing facilities
- shredders
- secure fax facilities
- confidential internal postal systems
- secure e-mail
- restricted access to any common pools of documents?

Remember, as an employee it is your duty *not* to discuss your employee's business details with anyone else.

The personal computer

Although it is in no way a requirement that this qualification is gained using a personal computer (PC), it is likely that the majority of candidates will do so. This computer may be operating as a stand-alone (single) computer or might be part of a network. For much of the qualification, and indeed for the majority of users, for most of the time it is not important which it is.

You will be using a wide range of different application packages, usually decided by company or department policy. Again it should not make any difference to your work for this qualification as long as the particular setup is capable of offering you the opportunity to carry out the required activities. It is not a requirement that you produce all your evidence using the same equipment or software. What is important is that you know what equipment you are working with and are aware of which packages and versions of the software you are using.

The first thing you need to do is find out some technical information about your working environment, often referred to as the specification. In order to do this you will complete a computer specification checklist given at the end of this chapter. The following explanation will take you through it and discuss the terminology.

Main components of the computer: hardware

Processor

This is the part of the computer that carries out all the instructions, and is often described in the model number; part of the description will include some information about its speed. For example, you may be using a 486 66 Mhz or perhaps a Pentium 160 Mhz machine. As models and speeds of processors change so frequently, you need to find out what is considered to be the current 'entry level' model. Computer magazines are a good source of such information.

CHECK IT YOURSELF

What is the make, model, processor and speed of the computer you will be using most frequently? Enter this information in section 1 of the computer specification checklist.

Memory

There are various parts of memory within a computer, each of which carries out a different function. The part that you, the user, need to be most aware of is called RAM (random access memory). This is the part of the computer that temporarily holds the programs and instructions you are using and the data you are inputting. This part of the computer's memory is usually 'volatile' – that is, when you switch the computer off anything that has not been stored will be lost.

Bytes

A unique unit of measurement is used for counting the size of various parts of a computer. This unit is called a byte. A byte is, generally speaking, the computer space necessary to hold a single character or code. Most of the time when describing the size of a computer's component you need to be talking in terms of thousands, millions and even thousands of millions of bytes. There are therefore a number of terms to describe these multiples. However, as computers are electronic and work in ons and offs, a different number base is used for counting – the binary system. The first multiple term used is a kilobyte (Kb). 1Kb = 1024 bytes but this is usually referred to as one thousand. The next multiple is a megabyte (Mb). 1Mb = 1048576 bytes (1024 × 1024) but this is usually referred to as one million. The third level of unit is the gigabyte (Gb). 1Gb = 1073741824 bytes but this is usually referred to as one thousand million, an American billion. For most PCs the size of the RAM is expressed in megabytes.

CHECK IT YOURSELF

What is the size of the RAM in your computer? Enter the answer on the computer specification checklist.

Storage

One of the important reasons for using a computer is that you can store your data and programs so that you can retrieve (recall) and amend them later. To do this you need to have a storage system. Most PCs will have two types of storage – a hard disk and a floppy disk drive.

The hard disk is the main, high-capacity disk which is usually permanently inside your computer. On this disk are stored all the programs and packages necessary to make your computer work, and you may also use it to store some of the data you wish to keep. This disk has a large capacity and this capacity is usually measured in megabytes or even gigabytes. Some computers, when connected to a network (see below), do not have their own hard disk drive but share the central resources.

The floppy disk drive has a much smaller capacity, usually 1.44 Mb, and this disk is not kept permanently inside the computer but is removed when not in use. This means that you can use different disks to store different sets of data. We will look at the organisation of disks later in the next chapter.

CHECK IT YOURSELF

What is the size of the hard disk (if any) in your computer? How many floppy disk drives do you have? Enter this information on the computer specification checklist.

Peripherals

This is the term used to describe all the parts that are added to the computer – that is, they are outside the computer and are plugged into ports (sockets) in the computer. There may be a wide variety of different peripherals attached to your computer depending on what it is used for (see Figure 2.1). The most likely ones are as follows.

Figure 2.1 Main computer peripherals include keyboard, mouse, VDU and printer

Keyboard

This is one of the main input devices and probably needs little explanation. However, it is important to note that there are some special keys on a computer keyboard.

There will be a Control (Ctrl) key and often there are two of these, just as there are two shift keys. They are both used for the same purpose, but it is convenient to have one on each side of the keyboard. The control is similar in concept and use to a shift key: it is used together with another key to send a different code to the computer. Then there is the Alternate (Alt) key which is another modifying key, like the shift and control keys.

Across the top of the keyboard you will find a set of function keys (F1–F12); these are used in different ways by different packages and programs. There is also the Escape (Esc) key which is again used in different ways by different programs.

Many keyboards have a numeric keypad on the right-hand side and also a set of cursor control keys. This keyboard is known as an extended or 102-key keyboard.

CHECK IT YOURSELF

Check what sort of keyboard you have and tick the box on the computer specification checklist.

Mouse

Most computers also have a mouse as an input device. This will have one, two or three buttons and a ball underneath which is moved across a flat surface to control a pointer on the screen. Using a mouse effectively is a skill in itself and one you need to acquire.

CHECK IT YOURSELF

Do you have a mouse attached to your computer? How many buttons does it have? Enter this information on the computer specification checklist.

VDU

One of the output devices you will have is a VDU (visual display unit). This might also be referred to as a monitor or screen – they all mean the same thing. This is used to enable the computer to communicate with you; what you input and the responses from the system appear on this device.

The VDU you are using will probably display a range of colours but can also be monochrome (black and white, green and black or amber and black). The quality of the display is described in terms such as VGA (video graphics array), SVGA (super VGA) or similar.

CHECK IT YOURSELF

Do you have a colour VDU? Find out the quality of your monitor and enter this information on the computer specification checklist.

Printer

You will probably have a printer either attached directly to your computer or, particularly if you are working on a network, one available for you to use but shared with other computers. Printing is still the most frequently used form of permanent output.

The technology of printing develops almost as quickly as that of the rest of computing. Most local printers (not on a network) attached to PCs are either laser printers or ink-jet printers. We will deal in detail with the technology of the different types of printers later. For now it will be sufficient for you to find out what type of printer you have and the speed it prints at. If it is a laser or ink-jet printer, the speed is measured in pages per minute (ppm). If you have another type of printer, the speed may be measured in characters per second (cps).

CHECK IT YOURSELF

What type of printer do you use? What is the make, model and speed? Can it print in colour as well as black on white? Enter this information in section 2 of the computer specification checklist.

Other peripherals

There may be a number of other peripherals attached to your computer, as there are many other types of input, output and storage devices. Some of the more frequently encountered ones include the following.

Storage

A CD-ROM is a compact disk which is capable of holding high volumes of data – this can only be created once and is therefore not appropriate for data that needs to change.

Figure 2.2 A CD-ROM in use

Input devices

- *Light pen* A pen-shaped input device which is pointed at the screen to make selections or to create images.
- *Scanner* An input device used to capture images and text from the printed page.
- *Graphics tablet* A flat board connected to the computer on which you can draw, with a special pen, images which are displayed directly on the VDU and can be stored in the computer.
- *Digitiser* A generic name for an input device used for converting data in its current form into digital data which can be processed by the computer; a scanner is a digitiser; a graphics tablet can be used as a digitiser.

Output devices

- *Sound card* A circuit board which enables high-quality sound to be produced on the computer – essential when using multimedia software.
- *Plotter* An output device used to produce high-quality graphics data – the image is created using a number of different-coloured pens which are picked up and put down by an 'arm' which moves across the paper.

CHECK IT YOURSELF

Find out what other equipment is attached to your computer and enter the details in section 3 of the computer specification checklist.

Main components of the computer: software

Having identified the hardware you use, it is equally if not more important to find out the specification of the software. There are two types of software – systems and applications.

You can now going to find out about the software you use and record this information on a software specification checklist given at the end of this chapter.

Operating system

The operating system is the set of instructions and rules which make the computer work. The operating system enables the computer to interpret each key you press, display it on the screen and make sense of it. It is necessary for the computer to be able to start up, to carry out your instructions and those of the software you buy, to save the work you do and to communicate with any attachments to your system such as disk drives, printers, plotters or devices to communicate with other computers.

The basic part of the operating system, that part necessary to start up the computer, is held permanently inside the computer in ROM (read-only memory). This is a part of memory you can only read from – you cannot change it by adding, editing or deleting anything. The rest of the operating system is normally held on the hard disk inside your computer. As new peripherals are added to your computer system, you need to provide operating system software to let your computer communicate with these devices.

An additional part of the operating system allows you to carry out utilities – these are activities which enable you to use the computer more effectively and to keep it in order (for example, making copies of files, deleting work that is no longer needed or moving files from one storage device to another). This type of activity is often referred to as 'housekeeping'.

When you buy a new computer, it may be necessary to install (set up) these parts of the operating system, but this is a simple and straightforward procedure which is mainly carried out by following instructions on the screen and responding to prompts for information. It is important to know which operating system you are using and which version number.

CHECK IT YOURSELF

What operating system do you have on the computer you usually work on? You need to find out the name of the company who supply it

and what it is called. What version number are you using at the
moment? Enter this information in section 1 of the software
specification checklist.

In recent years, computers have been made more accessible to general
users by the introduction of user-friendly 'environments'. This is done
by hiding the 'raw' operating system from the user and letting him or
her carry out many of the basic functions through the use of **WIMPs**
(**W**indows, **I**cons, **M**enus and **P**ointers).

Windows

A window (see Figure 2.3) is an
opening on your screen which
lets you view an activity. You
can have more than one window
open at any time and can
therefore look at and work on a
number of different activities at
the same time.

Figure 2.3   A window

Icons

An icon (see Figure 2.4) is an
image which is used to represent
a command or function you wish
to carry out.

   cut

   directory or folder

   print

Figure 2.4   Icons

Menus

A menu (drop down or pull
down) (see Figure 2.5) is a set of
options, usually used to give you
a choice from a number of
similar commands or functions.

Pointers

Pointers are the devices, such as
a mouse or a light pen (see
Figure 2.6), that let you more
easily use this environment. You
do not need to be able to use the
keyboard to issue commands to
the computer as you can select

File	Options	Window	He
New...			
Open		Enter	
Move...		F7	
Copy...		F8	
Delete		Del	
Properties...		Alt+Enter	
Run...			
E**x**it Windows...			

Figure 2.5   A menu

the icons and menus using a pointing device, although for many
functions this is slower than using the keyboard. As you become more
proficient you may prefer to use the keyboard for some functions
rather than pointing at the icons and menus.

For most computer users, the 'environment' they work in is called

Figure 2.6 Using a light pen

'Windows', but there are several other similar environments. For example, on the Apple Macintosh, Apple OS (the operating system) is always presented to the user as an 'environment'.

CHECK IT YOURSELF

Do you use an 'environment'? What is it called? Find out what version number you are using and enter this information in section 1 of the software specification checklist.

Networks

Although many people use their computer as a 'stand-alone' PC, it is very common for a number of PCs to be linked together to work as part of a network. There are many advantages if the computers are used in this way, including the following:

- The users on the networked PCs can communicate with each other.
- It will often only be necessary to have one copy of the software stored centrally which all the users can access – but see the section on licences (page 138).
- Peripherals, such as printers, can be shared by a number of users thus making better use of resources.
- Fast, high-volume data storage systems can be used with users being allocated their own space.
- Users can share data.
- Backup procedures (see page 67) can be carried out centrally.

There are a number of ways that computers can be networked together and, whilst you do not need to know a great deal about the technical side of this, it is useful to be aware of the basics of how your system is set up.

Just as the computer needs software to enable the various parts to communicate – the operating system – it is necessary to have software for the network to run. This software is known as the network software.

CHECK IT YOURSELF

Is the computer you usually work on part of a network? What network software is used to run the system? What version number are you using at the moment? If the computer is part of network, enter this information in section 1 of the software specification checklist.

Applications software

The software that is used to carry out the different tasks you do is called applications software. Some of this may be general-purpose packages, which are also known as 'generic' software. These are packages which are very general in the way they are used; it is for the user to set them up for a range of different uses. This term is usually used to refer to word processing, spreadsheet, database, drawing and desktop publishing packages.

Word processing

Word processing software enables the creation, saving, editing and printing of documents (see Figure 2.7). Modern word processing facilities include not only sophisticated text manipulation and presentation functions but also the facility for integration of data from other packages and the inclusion of graphical images.

Figure 2.7 Word processed document

Spreadsheet

Spreadsheet software is like a very large piece of paper that is divided into columns and rows, known as cells (see Figure 2.8). What you can see on the screen at any one time is just a small part of the complete spreadsheet available to you. Calculations, using formulae, can be entered

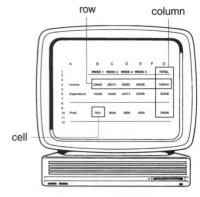

Figure 2.8 Spreadsheet screen

into cells and when the values in a cell are changed, all the formulae in the spreadsheet are automatically recalculated to give new results.

Database

A database gives you the opportunity to create an organised, structured collection of related data that can then be reorganised (sorted), selected and printed (see Figure 2.9). Queries can be made on the data to select the information before presenting it in a structured report.

Drawing

Drawing software enables you to create pictures and other images, often with facilities to use a wide range of colours and effects (see Figure 2.10).

Desktop publishing

Desktop publishing (DTP) software can be used to create documents by manipulating text and images (see Figure 2.11). Many word processing packages include basic DTP features whilst 'top of the range' DTP will produce copy ready for final printing.

Figure 2.9 A database report

Figure 2.10 Images created using drawing software

Figure 2.11 A DTP document

CHECK IT YOURSELF

What 'generic' software is available on the system you usually use? For each package find out the name of the manufacturer, the name of the package and the version number. Enter these details in section 2 of the software specification checklist.

In addition to using these generic packages, there may be a number of very specific applications that are carried out on the computer which need software that has been written to carry out these particular jobs. These pieces of software may have been specially written for an organisation or may have been purchased from a general supplier and customised for the particular organisation or user. Some examples of this sort of package are payroll, accounting or CAD (computer aided-design).

CHECK IT YOURSELF

Do you have any application-specific packages on the computer system you usually use? If so, what is the application? If it is an 'off-the-shelf' product, find out the name of the manufacturer, the name of the product and the version number. If it has been specially written, by whom? Enter these details in section 3 of the software specification checklist.

Computer specification checklist

Section 1: the computer	
Make	
Model	
Processor	
Processor speed	
RAM	
Hard disk	
No. of floppy disk drives	
Keyboard type	Extended (102) ☐ Standard ☐
Mouse	Yes/No No. of buttons:
VDU	Colour ☐ Monochrome ☐ VGA/SVGA
Section 2: the printer	
Type	
Make	
Model	
Speed	
Quality	Colour ☐ Black on white only ☐
Section 3: other devices	
Storage devices:	
CD-ROM	
Other	
Input devices:	
Light pen	
Scanner	
Graphics tablet	
Digitiser	
Other	
Output devices:	
Sound card	
Plotter	
Other	

Software specification checklist

Section 1: the operating system	
Name	
Version number	
Environment	
Version number	
Network software	
Version number	
Section 2: applications software	
Type of application	Word processing
Manufacturer	
Name	
Version number	
Type of application	Database
Manufacturer	
Name	
Version number	
Type of application	Spreadsheet
Manufacturer	
Name	
Version number	
Type of application	
Manufacturer	
Name	
Version number	
Type of application	
Manufacturer	
Name	
Version number	
Type of application	
Manufacturer	
Name	
Version number	

Software specification checklist (continued)

Section 3: application specific	
Specific application	
Manufacturer	
Name	
Version number	
Specific application	
Manufacturer	
Name	
Version number	
Specific application	
Manufacturer	
Name	
Version number	

3 Working with the equipment

Setting up equipment

When using equipment, it is extremely important that you follow the guidelines of the manufacturer and/or the suppliers. If the equipment is not set up according to instructions it may well not function correctly; it could also be unsafe! Make sure that you do not attempt to connect or disconnect anything for which you are not trained or which is outside your authority. If you have not done a task before, such as change a printer cartridge, get technical support and advice and always read the instruction manual first.

Setting up most equipment means not only the hardware but includes some software. When you connect a new printer to a computer it is usually also necessary to install the printer drivers, the software that controls the output. Different printers need different codes from the computer to achieve a particular feature. Again, make sure that you have authority to do this, that you follow any instructions fully and that you seek technical support if you are not sure of exactly what to do or have any difficulties during the process.

When you have finished using any equipment, make sure that you close down in the correct way. Whenever possible, you should exit from the software completely before switching off the computer. Failure to do so may result in loss of data or could leave temporary files on the system – these normally clear down automatically when you follow the correct procedures. Make sure you know which of the hardware should be turned off and how. This may be critical to other users of the system, particularly if you are working on a network. Don't switch off the network printer unless all the other users have finished as well, and you are authorised to do so.

Working with floppy disks

Most floppy disks need to be prepared before you can use them. This process is called *formatting*. You can buy preformatted disks, but you will have to pay more for them. It is a quick and easy task to format your own disks; the format command is provided as part of the operating system.

What does formatting do? It

- sets up the disk to be used in your type of disk drive (the number of tracks and sectors);
- creates the root directory;

- checks the writing surfaces of the disk and informs you of any damage;
- lets you give the disk a label (name); and
- deletes all existing data and file details.

Removable disks of all kinds are delicate items and need to be handled carefully. They can easily be damaged by

- excessive heat
- magnetic fields
- dust
- spilled drinks
- bending and crushing
- damp.

Disks contain valuable data and software, so you need to take good care of them. Some of this data may be confidential and will need to be stored securely. The disks that are supplied with software on them are often not copiable, and therefore need to be held in a secure and safe place. They should be

- clearly labelled and dated – write on the label before you put it on the disk or use a pen with a soft tip; and
- stored in a suitable box with a lock and kept in a safe place.

Working with printers

Different types of printers

There are advantages and disadvantages in using different types of printers.

Laser

Advantages
- High-quality print of both text and graphics.
- Reasonably fast models available.
- Quiet in operation.
- High-volume models available.
- Capable of printing on to acetates, envelopes and other specialist paper.
- Loading of paper is relatively simple.

Disadvantages
- Can usually only handle a maximum of A4,

Figure 3.1 Laser printer

standard-weight paper.

- Not suitable for multipart stationery.
- Use of heat and toner a potential health hazard.
- Relatively high running costs.
- Colour models expensive.

Ink jet

Advantages

- High-quality print of both text and graphics.
- Quiet in operation.
- Capable of printing on to acetates, envelopes and other specialist paper.
- Loading of paper is relatively simple.
- Reasonably inexpensive to buy.
- Good-quality colour models available which are not expensive.
- Some models can take A3 paper.

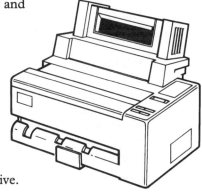

Figure 3.2   Ink-jet printer

Disadvantages

- Not suitable for multipart stationery.
- Relatively slow unless in 'draft' mode.
- Relatively high running costs.
- Some paper will absorb too much ink, reducing the quality of print.
- Some colour models do not print 'true' black.

Dot matrix (impact)

Advantages

- Relatively cheap to buy and run.
- Some very high-speed printers are available for high-volume printing.
- Capable of printing on multipart stationery, e.g. sets of invoices.
- Wide-carriage models are available for printing on large paper.

Disadvantages

- Noisy – inevitable with an impact printer.
- Only NLQ (near letter

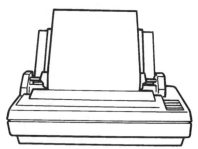

Figure 3.3   Dot matrix printer

quality) available – suitable only for internal reports and multipart forms.

- Capable of only medium-quality graphics.
- Most models work only with continuous stationery.
- Correct loading of paper can be quite difficult.

Managing the printer

Working effectively with printers can be a time-consuming activity. Unlike most other parts of the computer system, they are almost always produced by a different manufacturer and therefore have to be set up to meet your particular system's configuration. The applications software you use will usually be supplied with a number of printer drivers – that is, programs that send the correct sequence of codes to the printer to enable all the print features to work correctly. You should find that the right one for your printer is available, but this is not always the case; it will depend on the model of the printer and the version of the software. It is not unusual to be running under a compromise setup which works most of the time, but can sometimes cause unexpected results.

Because the printer is external to the main system and therefore the link is potentially fragile, it is always a good idea to save your work *before* you send it to the printer.

You need to make sure that you know how to do the following:

- Locate the on/off switch – but remember this should not normally be used to stop a print run as it may cause a paper jam, cancel any software settings for the font or paper orientation, or clear all the print instructions from the print queue.
- Find out which port it is connected to – this will probably be called LPT1 or something similar.
- Check the computer-to-printer cable – it should not be in a tangle, have any kinks, cuts or any signs of damage through crushing. It should be securely connected at both the computer port and at the socket in the printer.
- Load the paper tray or feed for continuous stationery – paper for laser and ink-jet printers must be loaded the right way up (there should be an arrow on the paper's packaging to indicate this). Continuous paper should be properly clipped on to the sprockets.
- Clear a paper jam safely – make sure the printer is switched off first and that you do not let your hair or any scarves/ties, clothing or items of jewellery fall into the equipment. (**NOTE:** You need to know the correct procedures and have the authority to open up the printer. If you don't, ask the technician or your supervisor to show you what to do so that you can do it under supervision next time.)

- Change a toner or ink cartridge or printer ribbon safely – this may need to take place at the same time as general maintenance and cleaning. You need to know details about the printer to make sure you are using the correct cartridge or ribbon – the wrong one could cause serious damage. (See the note at the end of the point above about opening printers.)
- Connect to a different printer – if you are working on a network you will need to know the software commands. Sometimes a number of users will share a number of printers through the use of a cross-over or T-switch, and you will need to take the other users into consideration.
- Load letter-headed paper – which way up and which way round, and don't forget to take it out when you have finished.
- Use special paper and acetates. You must make sure that the correct paper or acetates are being used – the wrong type of acetate can cause an awful mess inside a laser printer! Paper that is too thick or the wrong size can jam inside the printer.
- Use sheets of labels. As with special paper, use the correct ones for your printer and check how to load them.
- Print on envelopes – most laser and ink-jet printers are capable of printing on to envelopes, and there is usually a special way to load them.
- Install a new printer driver – you will need to find out if you have authority to access the disk area where these are stored. Make sure you inform other users of the changes you have made and how to use them. Sometimes a different printer driver could change the layout of a document by altering the page breaks or margin settings, and it may also alter the fonts and special effects on a document.

Management of the area around the printer is also extremely important. Waste paper lying around the desk and floor is a potential health and safety hazard. Printers, or rather their users, always seem to generate far more sheets of paper than are wanted! There are many, mostly avoidable, reasons for this, including the following:

- *Printing multiple copies.*
  Check the printer – has someone forgotten to set it back to single copies?
- *Producing a blank sheet after each printout.*
  The software installation may be wrong – speak to the technical support person.
- *Unwanted printouts.*
  Did you really need three or four copies?
- *Incorrect printouts.*
  Did you proofread, spellcheck, etc., **before** printing?

Who is responsible for the use of the printer, and what is done with the waste paper? Do you recycle your computer paper? Many organisations specifically collect and process paper from computer printers. If your organisation just throws this paper away at the moment, find out about services available locally and write a memo with recommendations to your supervisor or manager.

As one of the organisation's 'computer experts', you need to make sure that you know where plain and letter-headed paper and labels are kept. It is quite likely that others in the organisation will come to you for assistance in loading different types of paper, unjamming the printer, etc., and generally for help in dealing with minor printer problems.

Using the fax

Fax machines are relatively simple to operate and most work in a very similar way, but you do need to familiarise yourself with all the basic operations. Fax machines can usually be set either to a fax or telephone setting, so make sure you know how to do this.

Before sending a message, make sure that

- the machine is switched on;
- the document feeder is correctly adjusted; and
- the machine is ready to transmit – make sure it is switched to fax.

So that the fax is always ready to receive messages, make sure that

- the machine is switched on;
- the machine is in the fax setting;
- there is sufficient paper in the machine; and
- the ink cartridge is replaced when low.

Make sure that the area around the fax machine is kept tidy and free from waste paper. Does your fax machine just feed the printed faxes directly on to the floor? Suggest the use of a basket or something similar for them to feed into. This will keep the area tidy and also reduce the chances of a fax being lost (see also Chapter 6).

Fault reporting

One of the most frequent complaints concerning our dependence on computers is that they are always going wrong. In fact this is not true, as very often the 'faults' are not problems with the equipment but arise because users do not fully understand how to operate them or what the messages mean.

As an 'expert user', you need to make sure that you are able to recognise a true fault. Much of this comes from experience, but quite a lot is obvious if you think it through. If you ask your technical support team what are the most common faults reported to them they will undoubtedly tell you about

- the printer not being connected or switched on;
- the monitor's contrast and brightness being turned right down;
- the network connection being unplugged; or
- the mouse with its ball removed

. . . and so the list goes on.

The other kind of 'faults' that often arise are brought about by lack of knowledge as to how the software works:

- The printer prints gibberish or one line at the top of each page because the wrong printer driver is being used.
- The user is out of memory because there are too many windows open at the same time.
- The pictures in a document are missing from the printout because there is not enough disk space to create the print image.

The resolution of many faults can be speeded up if clear and precise information is passed on to the technical support people. When you report a fault always make sure that you

- copy down any error message exactly as it appears on the screen;
- note down the exact sequence that gave rise to the fault;
- give the precise location of the equipment – the floor, room and which machine if there is more than one in the room;
- give clear details of the equipment – e.g. the make and model

number of the printer;
- give the date and time the fault occurred;
- report it to the right person – you may have different support for printers or network problems, for example; and
- alert support staff to any urgent deadlines to be met – they might be able to offer you access to an alternative computer or printer so that you can meet your deadline.

Design a fault report form that will give all the information your technical support staff need *and* help you to keep a record of how and when the fault has been dealt with. Keep it simple and easy to fill in, otherwise it won't be used.

Cleaning the equipment

All the computer equipment, and the complete workstation, needs to be kept clean and – particularly – free from dust. Some of the responsibility for this may well be with technical support staff, but the basic cleaning can be carried out by the user.

You need to make sure any cleaning materials you use are safe for you to handle. Read any instructions on the product before you use it and take care not to inhale fumes from cleaning fluids. There will usually be details on the packaging of any particular precautions necessary, such as the use of gloves. You must also make sure that the product is appropriate for the equipment – you can do more harm than good if you use the wrong cleaning substances. Always check in the manual, or with technical support staff, to find out any specific 'do's and don'ts'. Keep up to date with any new products by reading office equipment and computer magazines. And do make sure that any cleaning you do is carried out with the equipment switched off!

You may be expected to take responsibility for the cleaning of the following:
- *Disk drives* – this is similar to cleaning a music or video cassette. Floppy disk cleaners are available for running inside the disk drive, to clean the read/write heads and prolong the life of the drives, thereby reducing the risk of damage to your disks.
- *Mouse* – this is very prone to dirt, particularly the rollers that run on the ball. These can be cleaned using a cotton bud moistened with water; make sure you use a mouse mat to reduce the level of dirt and to improve the performance of the mouse.
- *Mouse mat* – this is only useful if it is kept very clean and free

from dust; a quick wipe-over once a week with a damp cloth can make all the difference.

- *Keyboard* – a wipe-over with a damp cloth on a regular basis will remove most dirt from sticky fingers.
- *Screen* – anti-static screen wipes are quick and can make a great difference to the quality of the display.
- *Cases* – a wipe-over with a damp cloth on a regular basis will keep them clean.
- *Desk top* – keep your desk top tidy, free from clutter and clean it regularly to ensure that it is dust free.

Do you know how much damage the spilling of a fizzy drink or cup of tea can do to a keyboard? The acid in a fizzy drink can completely destroy the electrical contacts in the keyboard; the milk or sugar in your tea are particularly sticky when dry and will stop the keys from working properly. If something is spilt on a keyboard you should

- turn off the equipment immediately;
- place the keyboard upside down; and
- notify technical support so that they can clean and check it.

CHECK IT YOURSELF

Are there rules about food and drink being brought near computers in your work area? Write a memo to your supervisor alerting him or her to the consequences of an accident with a drink.

You can use the time when you are cleaning the equipment to carry out some basic routine checks on cables, etc., to make sure they are in good working order.

Almost everything that is created using a computer can be stored in a file – the software you buy, the data you input, the letters and memos you type, and even most of the operating system that you use to make the computer work. These files are stored in directories or folders on a storage device.

Whatever computer system you are using, there will be a set of rules, controlled by the operating system, about the names you give to files and how you organise the storage.

If you are using an industry-standard PC, you will probably be using a version of MS-DOS (Microsoft disk operating system). If you are using a different operating system you will need to find out the rules that apply to your computer.

Filenames

Every file has to have a name. This name must be unique to the storage area, directory or folder. The name must usually consist of letters and numbers only – many of the other characters on a keyboard have a special meaning in a filename. Files created in the PC environment have two parts. The first part is given by the user and is usually up to eight characters long without any spaces; in Windows 95 you can have up to 255 characters and even include spaces. The end of the first part of the name is indicated by the use of the full stop (.). This can then be followed by a second part, sometimes called the extension or suffix. This consists of up to three characters and will often be given automatically to the file by the specific applications software, e.g. word processing documents often have a suffix of **doc**. The complete filename is recorded in a directory, or folder, and is used to access the file. The directory contains details about the file – usually the date and time it was created or last updated, where it is located on the disk and what size (in bytes) it is.

Directories and subdirectories

When a disk is first used in a computer it has to be set up. This is known as formatting (see Chapter 3). Part of the disk is set aside to hold the directory information necessary to locate the files on the disk. This is known as the root directory and is referenced by the drive letter, a colon (:) and a back slash (\). For example, the root directory of the first floppy disk drive is referenced by **A:**. As it is possible to have a large number of files on any one disk, it is extremely important to organise them into subdirectories so that you can find them easily.

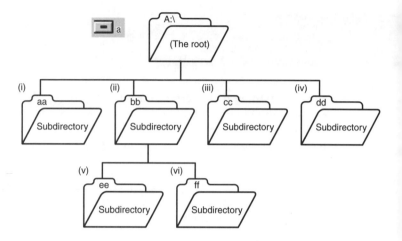

Figure 4.1 Disk structure chart

The system of subdirectories is hierarchical and is best understood through the diagram given in Figure 4.1. The paths in Figure 4.1 are written as (i) A:\aa, (ii) A:\bb, (iii) A:\cc, (iv) A:\dd, (v) A:\bb\ee and (vi) A:\bb\ff. Thus if all your documents relating to a sports and social club are stored on a floppy disk in subdirectory cc, you would find the minutes of the last committee meeting at A:\cc\mins298.

 CASE STUDY: Crink, Totem & Partners

Chris works in a solicitor's office and carries out work on the computer for the three partners (Anna, Peter and David) in the firm. In the past two years 73 files have been created and they are all stored in the root directory. This often causes great difficulty in finding a particular file when it is needed.

Chris has decided that it would be a good idea to organise the files into subdirectories. The files include word processing documents (with **doc** suffix), produced for each of the partners, and also spreadsheets (with **xls** suffix) for Peter and Anna.

1 Draw a disk structure chart similar to the one in Figure 4.1 to show how you might organise Chris's disk into subdirectories and show this to your tutor.
2 Figure 4.2 is a list of the files and the names of the owners that are on Chris's disk. Make a list for each subdirectory of the files you would put into it.

Filename	Owner	Filename	Owner	Filename	Owner
letta1.doc	Anna	reporta1.doc	Anna	letta13.doc	Anna
costp3.xls	Peter	reportd2.doc	David	lettp21.doc	Peter
costa2.xls	Anna	lettd3.doc	David	lettd21.doc	David
letta5.doc	Anna	lettp2.doc	Peter	costa12.xls	Anna
lettp7.doc	Peter	lettp5.doc	Peter	costa20.xls	Anna
costa4.xls	Anna	lettd4.doc	David	costp21.xls	Peter
lettd10.doc	David	reportp4.doc	Peter	lettd25.doc	David
reporta3.doc	Anna	reporta6.doc	Anna	lettd26.doc	David
costp4.xls	Peter	costa3.xls	Anna	reporta20.doc	Anna
lettd8.doc	David	lettp6.doc	Peter	lettp22.doc	Peter
reportp1.doc	Peter	reportp5.doc	Peter	lettp23.doc	Peter
letta15.doc	Anna	costp13.xls	Peter	reportd22.doc	David
letta20.doc	Anna	reportd21.doc	David	lettd28.doc	David
lettd23.doc	David	letta21.doc	Anna	letta24.doc	Anna
reportd18.doc	David	letta23.doc	Anna	lettd29.doc	David
lettd24.doc	David	costa22.xls	Anna	costa23.xls	Anna
letta26.doc	Anna	lettd27.doc	David	reporta22.doc	Anna
reporta21.doc	Anna	reportp23.doc	Peter	lettp25.doc	Peter
costp22.xls	Peter	letta25.doc	Anna	letta27.doc	Anna
lettd30.doc	David	reportp24.doc	Peter	reportd24.doc	David
lettp26.doc	Peter	reportd25.doc	David	costa24.xls	Anna
lettd31.doc	David	costa25.xls	Anna	lettp27.doc	Peter
reporta23.doc	Anna	costp23.xls	Peter	lettp28.doc	Peter
lettd32.doc	David	reporta24.doc	Anna	lettd32.doc	David
costp24.xls	Peter				

Figure 4.2 Files and their owners

CHECK IT YOURSELF

Is the storage system you use at work or in college organised into subdirectories?

It would be a good idea to keep all the files you are going to use as evidence for your qualification separate from any of your work or exercise files. Find out from your tutor or supervisor how to set up directories on your system and create a subdirectory for each type of file (word processing, spreadsheet, database, picture). You may decide as your evidence collection progresses to amend this structure.

Now make a record of this using a disk structure chart similar to the one in Figure 4.1 (you may need to modify this to meet your particular system). Place this in your evidence portfolio.

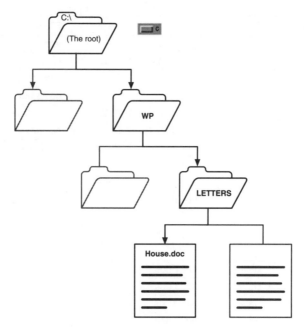

Figure 4.3 Accessing a file through a path

To access a file in a subdirectory you need to reference it through its path. The path is the way through the directory tree to where the file is. For example, if you are currently working in the root directory of disk Drive C and need to access a file called **House.doc** which is stored in a subdirectory called **LETTERS** which is itself in a subdirectory called **WP**, the path is **C:\WP\LETTERS\House.doc** (see Figure 4.3).

 CASE STUDY: Crink, Totem & Partners

Write out the paths you have set up for the following:

1   Files belonging to Peter:

   • **lettp7.doc**
   • **reportp23.doc**
   • **costp21.xls**

2   Files belonging to Anna:

   • **eporta1.doc**
   • **costa12.xls**
   • **letta23.doc**

Data storage standards

Remember, the files that are created and stored whilst you are at work belong to the organisation. This means that they need to be accessible to authorised people within the organisation. Would your supervisor or a colleague be able to find a document you had created so that they could print a copy or make some amendments when you are on holiday or off sick or should you leave the organisation?

Data storage standards need to contain three things.

Filenaming conventions

There need to be guidelines or rules as to what names are given to files. When working with most operating systems this can be quite difficult. As you will now be aware, there are many rules and limitations about what names you can give to your files. You may also have found out how difficult it can be to find the file you want several weeks or months after you have created it.

CHECK IT YOURSELF

Are there guidelines or rules set down for the names you give to your files at work? Find out what they are. Who is responsible for setting these rules? Are they written down? Do they apply across the whole organisation or are they limited to a department or section? Are they reviewed? Enter this information in section 1 of the organisation standards checklist given at the end of this chapter.

If not, how do you decide on the names for your files?

Filing systems

There need to be guidelines or rules about where the files are stored. You know it can be almost impossible to find your files unless they are organised into subdirectories or folders but, like any system, it is important that others can find their way round your filing system as well as you.

CHECK IT YOURSELF

Are there guidelines or rules for the organisation of your computer-based filing systems where you work? Find out what they are. Who is responsible for setting these rules? Are they written down? Do they apply across the whole organisation or are they limited to a department or section? Are they reviewed? Enter this information on the organisation standards checklist in section 2.

Recording systems

Not only must these first two be adhered to but also the details of the files and the structure of your filing system need to be recorded. All systems require some sort of documentation. Just because data is held and organised on a computer does not mean that documentation is no longer necessary – in fact, in many respects it becomes more critical as most of your main filing system and data are electronically stored. It is often not as easy to scan quickly through a computer system to find the file you need as with one on paper.

Let us say that you create, on average, between 10 and 20 new files a day. After working for the organisation for six months you could have created over 2000 files! If you, or anyone else, wanted to find a document you created on your first day, where would you start?

Many of these documents may have been amended or updated and sometimes you could have kept different versions for reference purposes. How will you know which version to use? To avoid wasting a considerable amount of time searching through your filing system, it is important to maintain an easy-to-use recording system.

Large volumes of data and a considerable number of different files can be contained both online (stored on disks that are permanently connected to the computer) and off-line (stored on disks that need to be loaded). There need to be records so that they can be easily located. What if the owner is not in the office? What happens when someone leaves the organisation? External bodies such as auditors also need to be able to find them, and so on.

For some of these records you can use the computer to produce the information. Printouts can give directory details for all disks (Figure 4.4). A procedure is needed to specify how often these records are updated and where they are stored.

CHECK IT YOURSELF

Are there guidelines or rules at work for a recording system for your computer-based filing systems? Find out what they are. Who is responsible for setting these rules? Are they written down? Do they apply across the whole organisation or are they limited to a department or section? Are they reviewed? Enter this information on the organisation standards checklist in section 3.

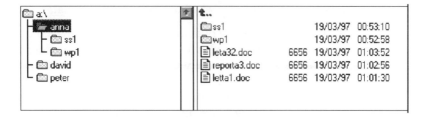

```
Volume in drive A has no label
Volume Serial Number is 15CD-0E29
Directory of A:\ANNA

.            <DIR>          19/03/97     0:51
..           <DIR>          19/03/97     0:51
WP1          <DIR>          19/03/97     0:52
SS1          <DIR>          19/03/97     0:53
LETTA1   DOC        6,656   19/03/97     1:01
REPORTA3 DOC        6,656   19/03/97     1:02
LETA32   DOC        6,656   19/03/97     1:03
       7 file(s)            19,968 bytes
                           603,136 bytes free
```

Figure 4.4   Disk directory printouts

Housekeeping

As with any filing system, it is necessary for your computer files to be maintained on a regular basis. It is very easy for large numbers of unnecessary files to be stored on your disks and to occupy considerable amounts of disk storage. The process of looking after your disk storage systems is known as housekeeping.

The main functions you will need to be familiar with to do this are those for *creating directories, copying, deleting, archiving* and making *backups*.

Backup procedures

In every computer environment, at work or at home, it is important that you keep backup copies of both the software on the system and of your work. Backup copies are kept for security reasons. The data that is stored on the main computer system will usually be 'live' data – that is, it is currently in use. It will include things like budgets that are being amended and/or monitored, ongoing correspondence which will still need to be referred to, minutes of meetings, etc.; in other words, the day-to-day work of the office. If this was 'lost' it would undoubtedly create extra work and could cause considerable disruption to the smooth running of the department or section of the organisation.

There are many reasons why you might lose your data:

- Floppy disks are very delicate and can be damaged quite easily.
- If the power goes off whilst the read heads are in contact with the hard disk you can experience what is known as a 'disk crash' and the whole disk may be completely destroyed.
- There are many viruses which can be brought into your computer that can destroy or corrupt your data.
- It is very easy to delete files by accident, but it can be very difficult to get them back.
- Unauthorised users may access files and accidentally or maliciously tamper with the data.

The *copy* command lets you make an exact copy of one or more files. However, this is limited in its use, particularly when the files to be copied are larger than the space available on a removable storage disk as it does not let you split a file between two or more disks. However, there is a pair of commands specifically designed to assist you with this procedure: one to make the backup copies and the other to restore the data should the original files be damaged or lost.

The *backup* command makes a copy of the files on to a numbered set of disks, prompting for the next disk as required. It does not, however, create readable or directly usable copies of the files. The usual way a backup command works is to create on each disk two files, one containing the data from the files and the second, often called a control file, identifying the names, sizes and creation dates of the files and also details of the sequence of the disk in the backup procedure.

The second command in the pair enables you to *restore* some or all of the data from these disks. It uses the information in the control file to find the data and to prompt you through the process as it restores the data from each disk.

These commands will usually allow you to carry out the backup procedure in a number of different ways. You can back up or restore

- all the files in the directory;
- all the files in the directory and any subdirectories of that directory;
- only those files that have been updated or created on or after a specified date/time; and
- only those files updated or created since the last backup.

During the process you can

- overwrite all previous files; or
- add files to those already on a backup disk.

In many organisations, particularly when working in a network environment, some of these procedures will be carried out centrally.

Find out what the backup procedures are where you work. Does this ensure that your data is secure? Are you responsible for any aspects of these procedures?

As the files you use as evidence for your qualification are extremely important, it would be a good idea to carry out your own backup procedure for them.

Write a brief description of the backup and recovery procedures for the organisation where you are working and also describe what you do to ensure the security of your NVQ evidence files. Place a copy of this in your evidence portfolio.

Archiving data

Archived files are not held for the same purpose as backups. Backup copies are held as security copies in case something happens to the originals. Archive copies are kept of files no longer needed in the main working environment but where a copy needs to be stored for reference or possible use in the future. It is quite common to keep electronic copies of old correspondence 'off-line' – many accounting records need to be kept for seven years.

As these files are not going to be used regularly it does not make sense for them to be in the active working environment. They would need to be maintained and backed up if they were kept there and would occupy expensive, online storage space.

If you have carried out activities you need for your 'evidence' but which are no longer needed for your work, it is best to archive them so that you still have them in electronic form but so that they do not occupy valuable 'online' storage space.

There are a number of different systems for storing archive copies of files. In its simplest form they are copies which are held on some form of removable storage system. This could be floppy disks, tape cartridge, micro-fiche or even CD-ROM.

 CASE STUDY: Crink, Totem & Partners

Chris has now learned how to carry out housekeeping and wishes to 'tidy up' the hard disk. All the files that have a number of less than 20 in them are from previous years' work and do not need to be kept online. As 'hard copies' of all letters are in the paper files, it is not necessary to keep the out-of-date electronic files at all. However, the reports and spreadsheets need to be kept for at least five years.

Make lists of

1 all the files to be deleted; and
2 the files to be archived on to floppy disk(s).

Discuss your decisions with your tutor.

CHECK IT YOURSELF

What procedures do you or your organisation carry out for archiving data? Write a brief description of these procedures and place it in your evidence portfolio.

Documentation

Backup and archiving procedures must have permanent records to enable them to function correctly. Backup details need to be logged and tapes or disks need to be labelled appropriately. You need to know when the latest backup was taken and what updates have taken place if you are going to be able to restore your records in the event of some form of disaster.

CHECK IT YOURSELF

Find out what the documentation procedures are in your working environment for online data, backup systems and archived data. Add this detail to the notes you have made about the main procedures.

Organisation procedures

A whole range of activities associated with computer-based work are tasks that need to be carried out on a regular basis, always in the same way and in accordance with a set of guidelines. To ensure that all staff who might be responsible for these activities know exactly what needs to be done, many organisations will have set written procedures.

Figures 4.5 and 4.6 show examples of guidelines for file storage in one organisation. We have already looked at a number of such activities in the sections on housekeeping and working with data. You may already have copies of the following procedures:

- backup and restore
- archiving
- recording of online data.

Within an organisation, these procedures may all be written in a similar way. Just as it is easier to learn to use another software package if it uses similar menus and terms to one you already know, so is it helpful to present all the procedures in a similar way.

Looking after your evidence

You will need to check what the commands are for your operating system or environment. As this is a fundamental part of working with computers make sure you are really confident about using these commands.

Set aside a time at least once a week to carry out the housekeeping of the disks and files that contain the evidence for your qualification, or it will become such a large task that it won't get done. There are a number of tasks that should be done on a regular basis:

- *Delete* all files that are no longer needed.
- *Move* all files into the right subdirectories – there always seem to be some in the wrong place no matter how careful you are at the time of creating them!
- Carry out *backup* procedures.
- *Archive* files that are no longer needed in the main work area.
- *Record* all these activities.

File storage guidelines

It is the responsibility of all computer users to ensure that their work is correctly saved and stored on the appropriate storage system. All access points (terminals) are provided with access to the company's network and also a local hard drive.

Local hard drive
The maintenance of data stored on the hard drive is entirely the responsibility of the users.

It is recommended that:

* each user stores work in a separate subdirectory/folder
* shared files are stored in a department/section subdirectory/folder
* a designated person has responsibility for operation of the backup procedures
* a departmental standard for filenames is operated
* individual users have responsibility for archiving long-term data
* individual users have responsibility for managing own data.

Department/section network areas
The maintenance of data stored in the network is primarily the responsibility of the **owner** department.

It is recommended that:

* a designated person within the department has overall responsibility for maintenance of the network area
* a departmental directory/folder structure is established and maintained
* a departmental standard for filenames is operated
* the department has responsibility for archiving long-term data - any data that has not been accessed for more than three months will be deleted from the system.

Central Computer Services will carry out routine backup procedures on a **weekly** basis. It is **strongly** recommended that the department carries out more frequent backup procedures.

Restore procedures
Requests for restoring data on the network must be made in writing to Computer Services. This must include details of the network area, directory path, filenames and date last modified.

Figure 4.5 An organisation's file storage procedures

Administration Department
File storage guidelines

It is extremely important to ensure that all data storage systems are maintained and that adequate records are kept within the department. The data that is held on the company-wide network is **more** secure than that held on the local hard disk. All work of a confidential nature should therefore be stored on the network.

Department network areas

Each member of staff has a secure, passworded area on the network and will be required to change the password at least every 30 days. Passwords should **never** be disclosed to anyone else. All members of the department also have access to a department area for storing shared data. The password for this area is changed by the office manager every 25 days and notified to all staff in the department.

- The **department area:** within this there are directories for each of the members of staff (staff member's name). If you need to subdivide your data further, you **must** notify the office manager of the name and purpose of the folder.
- For own **separate area:** within this the individual is responsible for setting up an appropriate structure.

Local hard disks

As the three computers in this section are used by all staff within the department, data needs to be organised to ensure that access to required files is straightforward and that other users are not likely to damage files accidentally.

- For **shared data:** the directory **Admin** has been set up. Within this there are directories for each of the members of staff (staff member's name). If you need to subdivide your data further, you **must** notify the office manager of the name and purpose of the folder.
- For own **separate data:** each member of staff has a directory based on his or her name. Within this, the individual is responsible for setting up an appropriate structure.

Filenames

All filenames should include the initials of the owner and clearly indicate the content of the document. All files kept on either the network or the local hard disk should be entered on to the disk log sheet. This must include the filename, the author, the date created and a clear description of content.

Archiving

All work that is no longer required online (either on the network or the local hard drive) should be deleted or archived on to floppy disk. All data on archive disks should be recorded on archive log sheets. Data in the network area that has not been accessed for more than three months will be deleted by Computer Services – make sure that it has been archived if it is needed.

Departmental backups

Computer Services will back up network data on a weekly basis.
The office manager will carry out network backups of modified files **only** for the **department** area on a daily basis (at 5.15 pm). It is the responsibility of individual owners to take more frequent backups of their own areas. The office manager will ensure that a full backup is taken of all the local drives weekly. It is the responsibility of individual owners to take more frequent backups of their own areas. All records of departmental backups will be kept in the department general office.

Restore procedures

Requests for restoring data on the network must be made in writing to Computer Services. This must include details of the network area, directory path, filenames and date last modified. Data can only be restored to the local hard disk with the authorisation of the office manager.

Figure 4.6 A department's file storage procedures

Organisation standards checklist

Section 1: filenames	
Is there a set of guidelines?	Yes ☐ No ☐
Who is responsible for setting them?	
Are they written down?	Yes ☐ No ☐
Are they for the whole organisation or the department?	Organisation ☐ Department ☐
Is there a system for review?	Yes ☐ No ☐
Section 2: filing systems	
Is there a set of guidelines?	Yes ☐ No ☐
Who is responsible for setting them?	
Are they written down?	Yes ☐ No ☐
Are they for the whole organisation or the department?	Organisation ☐ Department ☐
Is there a system for review?	Yes ☐ No ☐
Section 3: recording systems	
Is there a set of guidelines?	Yes ☐ No ☐
Who is responsible for setting them?	
Are they written down?	Yes ☐ No ☐
Are they for the whole organisation or the department?	Organisation ☐ Department ☐
Is there a system for review?	Yes ☐ No ☐

5 Working with data

Computer systems for most users centre around the input, processing and output of data. It (the data) is at the heart of the organisation. When working with data there are three main areas to consider:

- quality and accuracy
- integrity
- security.

Quality and accuracy

How often have you heard someone say 'the computer's got it wrong' or 'it's due to an input error'? As organisations, and indeed our lifestyles, become more and more dependent upon computer systems, this excuse becomes less acceptable. The methods of inputting and processing data are more sophisticated and more 'user-friendly', and this should mean that the quality and accuracy of the data improve. Most desktop generic software packages have a range of built-in checking facilities such as spelling checkers, but there is still considerable scope for mistakes to be made.

 CASE STUDY: Duke's Designs

Claude Duke is concerned about the quality of some of the data that is entered into the computers in his business and needs some ideas on what can be done to improve the situation. Below are three fairly typical problems that have arisen in the past few weeks:

1 The company's financial statement has been sent out to the board with the data figures for June and July the wrong way round.
2 A spreadsheet had been produced showing next year's budget. Some revisions had been made the day after the initial input, but the earlier version has been sent out by mistake.
3 A work-experience trainee on placement from the USA has been working in the general office. She has extremely good word processing skills and has produced the 'copy' for the printers for next year's catalogue. However, the whole document uses US spelling.

Listed below are three simple, basic techniques for improving the quality and accuracy of data. Match the solutions to the problems:

a Use of a spelling checker.
b Proofreading before dispatching.
c Using the automatic system date facility.

Integrity

Integrity of data refers to the correctness of the data throughout its life in the system. To ensure this, the following are needed.

1 **Adequate checks for validity and accuracy at point of entry**
   - *Verification of data* – this involves checks to make sure that the data is entered accurately. (For example, the data is entered twice into the computer by different people, the two versions are compared by the computer and any data with differences is rejected for checking and re-input.)
   - *Capture of appropriate data* – you should collect and store the data in the best way so that it will not need processing just to keep it current. (For example, date of birth rather than age, as the latter becomes incorrect as time goes by.)
   - *Batch totals* – these are particularly important when handling numeric, mainly financial, data. (For example, the total value of a set of invoices is calculated and entered at the start of the input process. As each invoice is input the computer keeps a running total of all invoices. When the complete set (batch) has been input the computer compares the input total with the calculated total and will only accept the batch if the totals match.)
   - *Validation of data* to make sure that it is an allowed value or response. (For example, the payroll system may be set up to accept only a range of values as no one has a salary above or below a certain limit, or, to make sure that only the correct names of the departments can be entered, they are selected from a 'pick list'.)
   - *Check digits* are extra digits, usually in an account number, which are based on the numbers in the account number and their sequence. If any number is entered incorrectly, or the numbers are entered in the wrong order, then the check digit will indicate that this is not a valid account number. (For example, your electricity or telephone account number has an additional digit which ensures that if any one digit of the code is entered incorrectly it should be identified as an error *before* you get the bill! This doesn't mean that the bill is correct but it does mean that the bill is sent to the right person.)
   - *On-screen checking* – that is, visual checking (proofreading). (For example, when your account number is entered, your name is displayed on the screen for the operator to check before continuing with the rest of the input.)

2 **Adequate controls throughout processing to ensure that the data is not accidentally altered or destroyed during processing**
   - *Control totals* are produced by the system at various stages of a process and should be checked manually as well as by the

system to identify any errors or corruption of data. (For example, in a cheque printing system, during the first stage of the process which involves identifying those suppliers for whom cheques are to be printed, the total value of all cheques will be calculated together with the total number of cheques. This control information will be printed and also passed on to the next stage of the process. As the cheques are printed, a running total will be made of the values together with a count of how many cheques. These second process control totals will be compared by the computer at the end of the process but should also be printed for a manual check.)

- *Check sums* are similar to check digits and are used to ensure that the numbers and sequence of numbers are not corrupted as the data is passed from one process or system to another. (For example, all the retail outlets of a chain store send their sales data through a communications link to the head office every evening after close of business. A mathematical formula is applied to this numeric data and from this an additional item of data (the *check value*) is derived. When the data is sent to the central computer system this additional item is also sent. When the data is received the same formula is applied and the two check values are compared to make sure they are the same. If they are not, the receiving computer can send a message requesting that the data be sent again as there is apparently an error.)
- *Backup and recovery procedures* (see the section on housekeeping in Chapter 4).

However, all that any of these systems can do is

- reduce the likelihood of input errors by the operator;
- reduce the chances of internal, computer errors – the computer software is still only as good as the quality of the programs;
- reduce the probability of processes being omitted or forgotten, by working to agreed procedures; and
- alert the user to errors that are encountered so that they can be responded to.

No amount of computer validation and checking removes the responsibility for the integrity of the system from the operator, user and ultimately the manager. When an error is identified, it needs to be acted upon.

An error might be simple and straightforward and within the immediate authority of the operator; if an account code has been entered incorrectly (for example two digits have been transposed – 12435 was entered instead of 12345) this can easily be rectified by re-entering the numbers in the correct sequence.

The error might have arisen, however, from outside your area of work or responsibility; it would be extremely unlikely that you would be authorised to decide what the correct data should be when entering data into the payroll system. If the value input for a new member of staff's salary has been rejected by the system as greater than expected (possibly because the annual salary has been put on the input document rather than the monthly amount), you would need to record this error and take it to either your line manager or possibly the person who authorised the original document.

Security

Adequate controls are needed throughout systems to ensure only authorised access to the data. This can be achieved by the following:

- *Passwords* for systems, programs and data. (For example, where you use a computer at work your password will probably give you access to the main set of programs such as word processing and spreadsheet packages, but only if you work in the Finance Department can you also access the accounts system, and only if you are responsible for managing the department can you also access budget data.)
- The regular *changing* of user *passwords*. (For example, in most organisations the system will automatically prompt you after a set number of days to change your password.)
- *Communications controls* to ensure that only authorised people can connect to the computer from an external link. (For example, a system known as 'dial-back' is used by many organisations. When a user – for example a home worker or one using a portable telephone – connects to the computer, the system knows from the user's log-in and password who they are and will have details of the authorised user's phone number. The link is immediately disconnected and the computer 'dials back' to the external system from which they will be connecting.)
- Access on a *need-to-know* basis – this means that access is denied to everyone unless they are positively identified as needing access to that system or data. (For example, the organisation may require that all password levels have to be requested in writing by the user with a description of why he or she needs the data. This then has to be countersigned by the line manager.)
- Ensuring that visitors to areas where there are computer screens are not able to view the data. (For example, careful consideration needs to be given to the positioning of equipment, particularly in areas where access is not restricted; users need to follow procedures about exiting from software, particularly where sensitive data may otherwise be left visible on the screen.)

CASE STUDY: Duke's Designs

Zeena works in the accounts section, processing invoices and general accounts data. She is aware that a number of her colleagues 'share' passwords with each other. They do this mainly so that they can help each other out when there are tight deadlines to be met. However, Zeena is also aware of at least one *former* colleague who still visits occasionally and who could gain access to the system.

She is concerned about the potential for a breach of security but also aware that this situation must be handled carefully as regards her colleagues. She has decided that she must do something about this but would rather not get her colleagues into trouble unnecessarily.

It is clear that the main reason for this problem is that the organisation does not have an appropriate system or set of procedures. One answer would be to introduce a system that required all users to change their passwords regularly, for example every 20 days.

Write a memo for Zeena to send to her supervisor, tactfully putting forward this proposal, identifying *potential* weaknesses in the system, without referring to the practice of her colleagues.

Presentation of data

Document layout

Whatever kind of document you are producing, a whole range of layout and presentation decisions need to be made. Although there will be slightly different ways of achieving these layout effects, most modern word processing, database, spreadsheet and desktop publishing packages will enable you to control the presentation of your documents.

The page

Depending on your printer and its ability to handle different sizes of paper, you will be able to select the following:

Paper size
If you are using a laser printer or ink-jet printer it will usually be A4 (8.27 × 11.69 in or 21 × 29.7 cm) but may also be Legal (8.5 × 14 in) or Letter (8.5 × 11 in). You may also be able to print on a range of different sizes of envelopes.

Paper orientation
Most printers are able to handle printing on the paper in either portrait or landscape (see Figure 5.1).

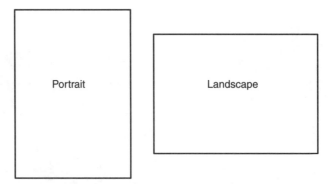

Portrait

Landscape

Figure 5.1 Paper orientation

Margins
The usable area of the page on which you can place the main part of your document is controlled by setting the size of the four margins – top, bottom, left and right (see Figure 5.2).

Headers and footers
A *header* is text that appears in the header zone defined by the top margin. It appears at the top of every page.

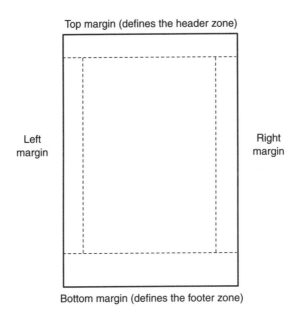

Top margin (defines the header zone)

Left
margin

Right
margin

Bottom margin (defines the footer zone)

Figure 5.2 Margins

A *footer* is text that appears in the footer zone defined by the bottom margin. It appears at the bottom of every page.

Headers and footers can be set up so that they are different for odd and even pages of a document or different on the first page of a document. It is also possible to have a number of different sections to your document and for the header or footer to change for each section.

Best fit
This is a facility which can be used automatically to adjust the layout and presentation of the document so that the information can all be fitted on to the page or into a given area of the page.

Footnote
A footnote is text which is referenced in the main body of the document, often using a number, and then either printed at the bottom of the page or at the end of a section.

Page numbering
The software will usually let you specify whether you want the pages of a document to be numbered automatically and where this should be printed, in the header or the footer. You will also be able to include such controls as omitting the number on page 1, something you often wish to do particularly with letters, and starting to count the pages from a particular number. This is useful where the document is only part of the final product.

Date/time stamping
It is often very useful for a document to have the date and/or time that

it was created or last updated printed automatically, usually as part of a header or footer.

The paragraph

Justification

<table>
<tr>
<td>This is an example of *left-*justified text. The left margin is aligned but the right margin is ragged.</td>
<td>This is an example of *right-*justified text. The right margin is aligned but the left margin is ragged.</td>
<td>This an example of text that has *full* justification. Both the left and the right margins are aligned. It is achieved by the software spreading the text to fit the margins by inserting additional *soft* spaces.</td>
</tr>
</table>

Lines and boxes

There will often be a range of ways in which you can highlight and draw attention to parts of a document. You will be able to draw lines and boxes and, even if you don't have colour printing facilities, you can using shading to produce a variety of effects.

The text

Font style

The shape and style of the text can be varied enormously. Most printers will support a considerable number of these fonts. Some are very plain and clear and therefore appropriate for business applications, whilst others are much more fancy and elaborate *(like this one which is called Brush Script)* and are very effective for less formal communications or possibly for posters and leaflets.

Font size

Not only can you use different fonts but you can also control the size. With printers capable of producing very high-quality print, it is possible to print very small, fine characters quite clearly but also to print very large letters. Most fonts are measured in points – the bigger the number the larger the character.

Text enhancements

As well as enhancing the way the text looks by using different fonts and sizes, it also possible to add emphasis to selected parts of the text. The three most commonly used forms of emphasis are **emboldening,** *italics* and <u>underlining</u>. It is of course possible to use a combination of these features to achieve different effects.

It is extremely important that you use these features appropriately and not excessively. Too many different types of enhancement and emphasis within the same document will only cause confusion and detract from the content of the document.

House styles

So that an organisation can have control of its image – the way it presents itself to the outside world – it is usual for certain rules and guidelines to be laid down about external communications. At its most basic level, this will probably include an organisation standard on how letters are to be laid out. Further to this, to maintain and foster a corporate identity, it is also quite normal to have rules and guidelines for internal communications.

Most organisations will have some form of logo, often based upon the name of the organisation and usually incorporating a graphic or image. These days this will often be held as a graphics file which is readily available to all computer users so that it can be incorporated into documents.

In some organisations there will be a set of guidelines as to which printer fonts and sizes are to be used for particular situations; in others, documents will be less formalised. There may be a different set of guidelines for in-house and external communications.

Letter layout

Something as apparently simple as how a letter is laid out is important for an organisation's image. There are many different ways of presenting a letter, and 'normal' practice changes. Quite often the changes are in response to the latest facilities available in the most recent release of the word processing software. Until word processors became commonplace, the justification of text could not easily be controlled and so text was always left aligned. With the general availability of high-quality laser printers with a range of fonts and sizes, the way text is emphasised has changed. For example underlining of text is far less popular than a few years ago, whereas the use of *italics* or **bold** is often preferred.

How do you write the date, and where is it placed? Most word processing systems are capable of inserting the current date automatically (or at least the date the computer calculates it to be!) and you can choose its format. Commonly used date formats include:

06/05/98; 06 May 1998; 6 May 1998; May 6 1998; 6-May-98

You should note, however, that conventions differ in North America, so a letter from New York dated 06/05/98 would indicate it was written on 5 June 1998!

Pages of documents can be numbered automatically and you can decide whereabouts on the page to place the numbers and what they should look like. Some organisations have a standard where the first page of a letter does not have a number (so a single-page letter will not be numbered) whereas others will include a page number on page 1 if there is more than one page. For letters it is usual to have page numbers somewhere in the footer of the page, either on the left, right or in the centre of the page.

Which font and size should you use? There will usually be a preferred, or even required, style. One thing is certain, however, and that is that above all else you need to ensure that you are *consistent*.

You need to make sure you know the organisation's conventions on

- use of letterheads
- addressing conventions
- bold/underlining, etc.
- paragraphs – justification/blocks
- page numbering
- date format and position (see Figure 5.3).

Figure 5.3 House style

Find out about the conventions for letters in the organisation where you work and enter the details in section 1 of the organisation house styles checklist given at the end of this chapter.

There will probably be a similar, although possibly less formal, requirement for internal communications such as memos.

Find out about the conventions for memos in the organisation where you work and enter the details in section 2 of the organisation house styles checklist.

Again, there will probably be some conventions in the organisation for the production of reports. They will, as with letters, be based upon consistency and the image the organisation wishes to present, and will probably include the following:

- Section and paragraph numbering systems. Most word processors enable you to number paragraphs automatically with a range of different systems to choose from (a, b, c or i, ii, iii or I, II, III or 1, 2, 3, etc.).
- Justification of paragraphs – this may depend upon whom the report is for and whether it is to be circulated internally only, or also to be distributed externally.
- Page numbering – as with letters there is a range of options. Reports may have the page numbers at the top or bottom of the page and will often identify how many pages there are in total (i.e. Page 1 of 5).
- Drafts – how should the draft status of a document be indicated? For example, is the word 'draft' include as part of a header and should it be in capital letters? Many organisations print reports in double-line spacing whilst they are in draft format, so that revisions can more easily be indicated. Reports will usually need to include a date. Should this appear on every page? Possibly in the header or footer?

Find out about the conventions for reports in the organisation where you work and enter the details in section 3 of the organisation house styles checklist.

Organisation house styles checklist

Section 1: the letter	
Organisation letter head	Yes ☐ No ☐
Preprinted stationery?	Yes ☐ No ☐
Available as a graphic image?	Yes ☐ No ☐
Specified font and size	Font: Size:
Page numbering convention	
Date format and position	
Emphasis	
Paragraphs – justification/blocks	
Section 2: the memo	
Standard format	Yes ☐ No ☐
Preprinted stationery	Yes ☐ No ☐
Specified font and size	Font: Size:
Date format	
References – footers	
Section 3: formal reports	
Standard format	Yes ☐ No ☐
Specified font and size	Font: Size:
Paragraph numbering systems	
Paragraph formats – justification	
Page numbering	
Draft layouts, e.g. line spacing	
Headers and footers	
Date formats	

6 Working in the electronic office

Identifying and prioritising tasks

It is likely that most of the tasks you will be expected to do will be generated by other people. Much of the work will be routine activities that you will be required to carry out on a regular basis. For example, you may need to enter the regional sales figures each week into a spreadsheet and then send a printout to each of the regional managers. It would be your responsibility to make sure the changes are *accurate*, that the job is done *on time* and the task is *completed* by either printing it out and circulating the hard copy, or by sending an electronic version to those who need this information.

There are also likely to be times when your supervisor gives you a non-routine job to do. For example you may be asked to compose and word process a letter to a supplier enquiring about prices and delivery schedules of specific items.

When there are a number of tasks to be done, you need to organise your workload and decide your priorities. Sometimes it is not easy to decide which job should be done first. For jobs that you carry out on a regular basis it should be reasonably straightforward, as you know what is involved, you know how long it is likely to take and you will usually have a good idea as to how critical the completion time is. However, it is more difficult to assess non-routine tasks as they are, by their very nature, unpredictable. You may need to seek guidance from your supervisor when deciding priorities involving something that you do not do regularly and it may be even more important to alert the 'customer' if there are likely to be any difficulties with meeting deadlines.

For any work you do, you need to make sure that you have the authority to do it. You need to have authority to access the data and the software you need to use. If in doubt, check with your supervisor and/or the 'customer'. If you are given a piece of work to do which is outside your usual authority, make sure that your supervisor is aware of this and is able to support or assist you if required. Remember that you may not be able to ask your colleagues to help you in the way you usually do; you will need to take into account the confidentiality of the data and the nature of the task.

Accuracy is extremely important. If you are inputting a set of data, not only should you take care to enter the data correctly but you also need to make sure you are inputting it in the right place. Sometimes it may not be completely clear as to what you have to do. Don't 'have a go' and hope you've got it right – check what is required before you do it. If you are doing some complex or particularly lengthy work, don't wait until the end before checking that what you have done is right. Check after you have done a little – it could save you a lot of time.

Activities within the office can be greatly improved through the use of electronic equipment and facilities. Three main areas of activity are involved:

- document preparation and production
- document transmission (facsimile – fax)
- data transmission.

Document preparation and production

The 'heart' of this qualification is about applying your skills and knowledge to the activities and tasks carried out in an 'electronic office'. Unit 2 is the mandatory unit which covers the practical application to the working environment and includes activities that require working with text, numbers and graphics in the preparation and production of documents.

Text-based documents

Many documents are now produced in-house that would have been sent out to specialist designers and printers in the past, or may have been created through the use of more specialist software such as desktop publishing (DTP).

When producing such documents, you will usually be working to the requirements of your manager, colleague or other 'customer'. You will be required to produce these documents to meet their standards both in terms of 'house style' and general layout and presentation (see Chapter 5), and within the timescales they define.

In most organisations, letters, internal communications such as memoranda (memos), forms and reports are prepared using some form of electronic text processing facility, usually a word processing system. Modern word processing facilities have features way beyond those that would previously have been carried out on a typewriter.

The basic text processing facilities of wordwrap, editing, cutting and pasting, and tabulation have been greatly enhanced with a wide range of features such as the ability to carry out automatic numbering of paragraphs, use of bullets, applying spelling checkers in a wide range of languages, looking up words in a thesaurus to assist in the use of just the right word, and sophisticated line drawing and text presentation features.

Many of the uses of word processing, such as filling in forms, can be automated through the use of interactive macros which assist the user by prompting at each point in the process. Mailmerge facilities mean that standard mailings can easily be prepared for multiple recipients but each can have the look and presentation of individual correspondence.

Major advances in the quality and economy of printing have made many of these features possible. Laser and colour ink-jet printers are available for desktop use and can produce output close to the quality that was once available only on expensive printing equipment. To support this, word processing software offers a wide range of fonts and text enhancements to enable the user to produce impressive-looking documents.

CHECK IT YOURSELF

A very wide range of techniques and skills are needed to be an 'expert user' of text processing facilities. All full-feature software will enable you to produce highly complex and well presented documents.

The text processing checklist at the end of this chapter includes all the main features you need to be able to use in your particular software. As you progress towards your qualification, complete this checklist and include it in your evidence folder as supplementary evidence.

Graphical images

There are two main types of graphical images: vectors and bitmaps.

Vector graphics

Vector graphics are constructed using lines, and will typically be used for many technical applications as the resulting images are more precise and better able to be manipulated as objects. These are usually created using digitisers and graphics tablets, but can also be produced using programs to draw lines between Cartesian (x,y) co-ordinates.

There are specialist graphics packages for the drawing office, known as CAD (computer-aided design/draughting) (Figure 6.1). With these, engineering drawings of all types can readily be produced. Many of these can be used directly to control the manufacture of the designed item.

True three-dimensional images that can be rotated must be vector images. Computer games, where you move through a three-dimensional space and need to view objects from all directions, and virtual reality use this type of graphics.

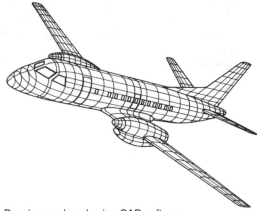

Figure 6.1 Drawing produced using CAD software

Bitmap images

Bitmap images are created in pixels and consist of blocks of colour. Images that have been created through a scanning process will be in this form. Most drawing and art packages produce images in this format (Figure 6.2).

Company logos, pictures to be included in leaflets and graphical representations of data will usually have been created in this way. As they are increased in size, so the smoothness of the lines may be reduced.

a
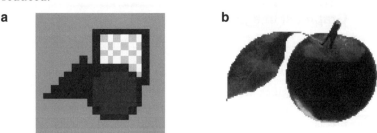
b

Figure 6.2 Bitmap images can be edited pixel by pixel (a) and produced using a paint package (b)

Many drawing packages enable the artistic to produce high-quality images and to save these in digital form. There is also a vast range of 'clip art' which can be bought or is provided free with software packages. Many popular images are available to enhance the presentation of documents. It is important to make sure, however, when you are using images you have not created yourself, either from 'clip art' or by scanning them in, that you are not breaking any copyright laws (see Chapter 8).

For those intending to complete Unit 7

To be an 'expert user' in the use of graphics creation software a wide range of techniques and skills are needed. All full-feature software will enable you to produce highly complex and well presented images.

The graphical images checklist at the end of this chapter includes all the main features you need to be able to use in your particular software. As you progress towards your qualification, complete this checklist and include it in your evidence folder as supplementary evidence.

Processing numerical data

One of the things computers have always been used for is to carry out calculations. They are capable of performing vast numbers of calculations in a very short space of time. Many of these applications involve the use of special software which has been set up to perform specific functions, such as accounting, complex engineering design calculations, production forecasting or even putting humans on the moon. However, we all need to be able to do much simpler calculations, both in our daily lives and in our work.

We all know how difficult it is to keep track of our money and to make sure there will be enough to meet our commitments. To do this using pen and paper, you would probably make a list of all the sources of

MY PERSONAL MONTHLY BUDGET				
	WEEK 1	WEEK 2	WEEK 3	WEEK 4
BALANCE IN MONEY IN Wages Other				
MONEY OUT Rent Electricity Food etc Entertainment Clothes Travel Other				
TOTAL IN TOTAL OUT BALANCE				

Figure 6.3 Layout for a monthly budget

money coming in, your pay cheques, benefits or grant, and then make another list of all your regular expenditure. You would probably want to look at this over a period of time, say four weeks, and so you might end up with something like Figure 6.3.

You would then need to write down the amounts of money, carry out all the necessary calculations (adding up and subtracting), possibly using a calculator. But then, what if you realised that you'd left something out, over- or under-estimated how much something cost, or just added it up wrongly? Your piece of paper could end up looking like Figure 6.4! A spreadsheet package will do all these things for you, and you can keep changing it until it is right.

MY PERSONAL MONTHLY BUDGET				
	WEEK 1	WEEK 2	WEEK 3	WEEK 4
BALANCE IN	21.23	60.93	130.63	-29.67
MONEY IN				
Wages	155.00	155.00	155.00	155.00
Other		~~30.00~~	30.00	
MONEY OUT				
Rent			225.00	
Electricity	5.00	5.00	5.00	5.00
Food etc	30.00	30.00	30.00	30.00
Entertainment	~~15.00~~	15.00	15.00	15.00
Clothes	~~40.00~~ ~~30.00~~	~~5.00~~	40.00	~~40~~
Travel	20.30	20.30	20.30	20.30
Other	15.00	10.00	15.00	15.00
TOTAL IN	176.23 ~~155.00~~	215.93	315 ~~285.63~~	125.33 ~~55.00~~
TOTAL OUT	115.30	85.30	345.30	85.30
BALANCE	60.93	130.63	-29.67	40.03

Figure 6.4 A worked-out monthly budget

All spreadsheet packages are set up like a very large piece of paper (far bigger than you will ever need), usually known as a worksheet. This is divided into columns and rows that form boxes, known as cells. What you see on the screen at any one time is just a small part of the available spreadsheet. The columns are likely to be numbered from A to ZZ and the rows from 1 to 999. You can enter data into any cell, and this data may be text or numbers. Calculations (worked out using formulae) can also be entered into cells and, when numeric values in a cell are changed, all the results from the formulae in the spreadsheet are automatically recalculated to give new results. These formulae, or rules, together with the column and row headings, define what is known as the *model* (Figure 6.5).

	A	B	C	D	E
1	My personal monthly bu	dget			
2					
3		WEEK 1	WEEK 2	WEEK 3	WEEK 4
4	BALANCE IN		=B24	=C24	=D24
5					
6	MONEY IN				
7					
8	Wages				
9	Other				
10					
11	MONEY OUT				
12					
13	Rent				
14	Electricity				
15	Food etc				
16	Entertainment				
17	Clothes				
18	Travel				
19	Other				
20					
21	TOTAL IN	=SUM(B4:B9)	=SUM(C4:C9)	=SUM(D4:D9)	=SUM(E4:E9)
22	TOTAL OUT	=SUM(B13:B19)	=SUM(C13:C19)	=SUM(D13:D19)	=SUM(E13:E19)
23					
24	BALANCE	=B21-B22	=C21-C22	=D21-D22	=E21-E22
25					

Figure 6.5 The model – this shows the layout with column and row headings and the formulae

Once you have set up the layout and rules for your calculations, you can enter and edit the numeric data to project results for different situations (Figure 6.6).

	A	B	C	D	E	F
1	My personal monthly budget					
2						
3		WEEK 1	WEEK 2	WEEK 3	WEEK 4	
4	BALANCE IN	21.23	60.93	130.63	-29.67	
5						
6	MONEY IN					
7						
8	Wages	155.00	155.00	155.00	155.00	
9	Other			30.00		
10						
11	MONEY OUT					
12						
13	Rent			225.00		
14	Electricity	5.00	5.00	5.00	5.00	
15	Food etc	30.00	30.00	35.00	30.00	
16	Entertainment	15.00	15.00	15.00	15.00	
17	Clothes	30.00		30.00		
18	Travel	20.30	20.30	20.30	20.30	
19	Other	15.00	15.00	15.00	15.00	
20						
21	TOTAL IN	176.23	215.93	315.63	125.33	
22	TOTAL OUT	115.30	85.30	345.30	85.30	
23						
24	BALANCE	60.93	130.63	-29.67	40.03	
25						

Figure 6.6 A set of values – this shows the results of the calculations with one particular set of data

Who uses a spreadsheet? The answer is almost anyone. A spreadsheet package is often used as a management tool to examine numerical data and to make 'what if' projections. It is used by accountants, sales and marketing executives, personnel departments, project managers and also for many general administrative and clerical tasks. Quite often the data entered into a spreadsheet has been extracted from another computer program (e.g. the accounting software) and then imported into the spreadsheet so that further calculations can be carried out.

As with all modern software, it is also possible to have considerable control over how the information is displayed and printed. You are able to adjust the orientation of the page, alter the margins so that you get the 'best fit' on the page, include headers and footers, control the justification of the text and apply many different types of enhancements such as lines, boxes, bold or italics, and use shading to highlight headings or important cells of information. You can also extract all or part of a spreadsheet to be used in another application such as in your word processed report (see below).

Because a spreadsheet is very versatile, it is an extremely flexible modelling tool that lends itself to a wide range of uses. All spreadsheet packages work in an almost identical way and have a set of reasonably simple, basic commands you need to be able to use.

However, to create a model that works well, you need to have a clear understanding of the factors to be included and the way in which it will be used. The most effective models are planned before they are entered into a software package. Some preparation at the design stage can reduce significantly the amount of correction needed later. The design of the layout is extremely important. You need to consider

- the format of the data;
- the information required from the model;
- the calculations and formulae that have to be applied to the data;
- how easy it will be to amend;
- how easy it will be to extract data for another application; and
- the way the results are to be presented.

CHECK IT YOURSELF

For those intending to complete Unit 6
To be an 'expert user' of data modelling software a wide range of techniques and skills are needed. All full-feature software will enable you to produce highly complex and well presented models.

The data modelling checklist at the end of this chapter includes all the main features you need to be able to use in your particular software. As you progress towards your qualification, complete this checklist and include it in your evidence folder as supplementary evidence.

Business graphics

Most businesses need to produce facts and figures about how the business is doing in terms of its profitability and in comparison with previous years. They may also wish to compare their financial achievements with those of their competitors. Whilst the accountants and financial wizards might like to see this information presented as columns of numbers, most people find it much easier to understand the situation at a glance if the figures are displayed graphically.

Charts and graphs can be produced from business data using a variety of software including some word processing packages, most spreadsheet packages and a range of charting programs. There are also packages which help you to produce organisation charts and diagrams.

Graphical display of data

There are a number of different ways of displaying data graphically. Which one you use depends on the type of data, and the image that is most appropriate and visually effective for the particular purpose. It is often helpful to create a rough sketch of what you want to see in the graph before you create it.

Bar (column) charts

A bar chart is used to display graphically the *frequencies* of a set of data. It is drawn with either horizontal or vertical bars of comparative lengths. Bar charts are particularly suitable if you want to compare different quantities over a period of time, or to display clearly the different amounts for a range of items.

An example of a vertical bar chart is given in Figure 6.7 showing how many (frequency) square kilometres of arable land in the UK were used for growing barley, oats and wheat in 1990. An example of a horizontal bar chart is given in Figure 6.8 comparing the value (frequency) in thousands of pounds of electrical equipment sales in the financial year 1997–98.

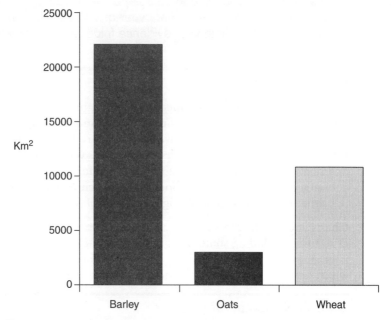

UK arable land growing grain – 1990

Figure 6.7 A vertical bar chart

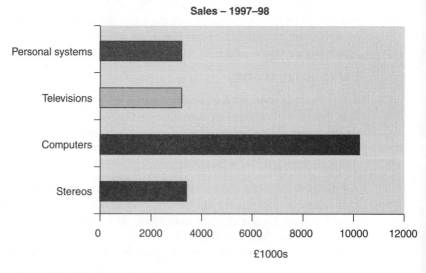

Sales – 1997–98

Figure 6.8 A horizontal bar chart

Pie charts

Sometimes you wish to display the relative frequencies of the data. This is done by calculating the frequencies as a share of the whole. This is done most often using percentages of the whole (each item's

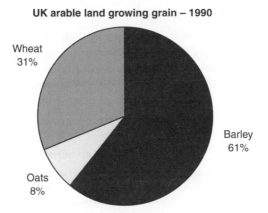

Figure 6.9 Pie chart of the data given in Figure 6.7

frequency divided by the total and multiplied by 100). Each frequency is represented as a portion of the whole pie – that is, as a percentage of the 360 degrees of a circle.

This type of chart requires relatively complex calculations and is not easy to draw when using pen and paper, but when using a computer all the hard work is done for you by the software! An example is given here of the data used for the bar chart in Figure 6.7, but showing each data item (barley, oats and wheat) as a percentage of the total land use (Figure 6.9).

The second pie chart shows the value of sales of electrical goods given in Figure 6.8 in the financial year 1997-98 as percentages of the total sales of the organisation. The labels for the segments have been included in a legend (Figure 6.10).

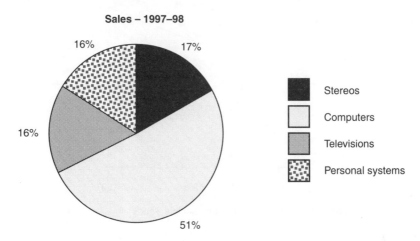

Figure 6.10 Pie chart of the data given in Figure 6.8

Line graphs

When you want to show a *trend* in your data, it is often best to use a line graph. This shows a number of points joined together by a line. Each data value is plotted and then joined by a line which shows the change visually. An example is the data for arable land used for the production of barley in the three years 1980, 1985 and 1990 represented in a line graph (Figure 6.11).

Use of arable land for growing barley

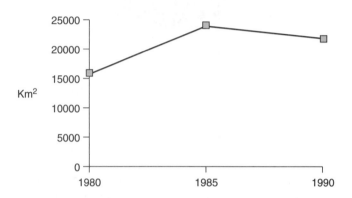

Figure 6.11   Line graph showing a single trend

Sales – 1995–97

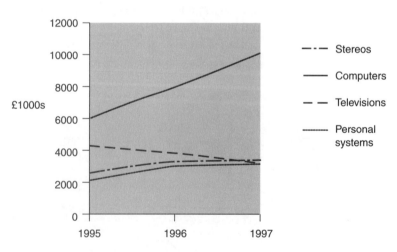

Figure 6.12   Line graph showing multiple trends

Line graphs can be particularly effective when a number of trends are displayed on the same graph. The example in Figure 6.12 shows the trends in the sales of each of the four categories of electrical goods over a period of three years. If you were the business manager, which product might you want to concentrate on, and which might you consider discontinuing?

CHECK IT YOURSELF

When displaying business data graphically, it is important that you use the most appropriate and effective type of chart. You will need to consider the content of the data, the purpose of the chart and by whom the chart is going to be used. For example, the accountant will want to be able to see exact values for the company's turnover, whilst shareholders may be more concerned with seeing at a glance the extent of the increase on last year's figures.

Which type of chart would you use for each of the following tasks? Put a ✔ in the box to indicate your choice.

	Bar chart	Pie chart	Line graph
1 The value of sales each month in the region during the past six months, for use at a meeting of sales managers	☐	☐	☐
2 Actual profit earned from items in the company's range of products, to be included in the financial director's report to shareholders	☐	☐	☐
3 The makeup of the workforce by age (five ranges) for the Annual Report	☐	☐	☐
4 The proportion of production costs accounted for by labour, materials, plant, power and distribution	☐	☐	☐
5 Income generated this year by each department in a firm of solicitors	☐	☐	☐
6 A comparison of monthly expenditure against budgets during the first three months of the financial year	☐	☐	☐
7 Fluctuations in the rate of exchange of the pound against the US dollar over the past four years	☐	☐	☐
8 The percentage of staff employed in each department	☐	☐	☐

Integration of text, data and images

Many documents, either for business or leisure purposes, can be improved and enhanced by the use of graphics or the inclusion of a set of data. A general newsletter distributed to all staff is more interesting to look at if it includes more than words; company reports are quicker to produce if the tables or figures do not need to be typed in again and can also be displayed as a graph; the invitation for all staff to the interdepartmental five-a-side football match will be more inviting with some pictures in it (Figure 6.13).

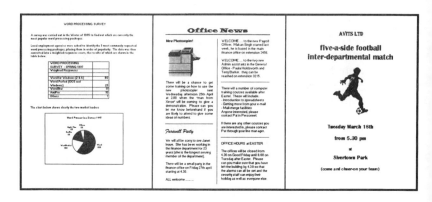

Figure 6.13   Graphics enhance any kind of text

Recently there have been considerable advances in software to help you integrate text, data and graphics within a document. Previously it was usually necessary to use specialist software such as a desktop publishing package in order to incorporate graphical images into a text document. In most instances these packages required a high level of specialist skills in order to achieve high-quality presentations. Now, most word processing packages can handle graphics in almost any format and have made this form of presentation accessible to all.

At the same time as software developments have been taking place, advances in the power of computers have kept pace. Many desktop computers are now capable of simulating 'multi-tasking'. This means that although you can only use one package at a time, it is possible to have a number of packages loaded into the computer's memory and for the user to 'switch' between them. With the ability to work on a number of different applications at the same time, the process of passing data between them has become much quicker. This is usually achieved by using a facility often known as the *clipboard*. This is a part of the RAM that is set aside as a special storage area. You can place a *copy* of the data, images, etc., on to it and then *paste* this into another document or file.

For example, you are creating a simple set of instructions for your colleagues on how to run the new software that has been set up. You want to include in your word processed document a 'screen-shot', or picture of the screen, to improve the clarity of your description:

- When working in Windows, you can take a 'screen-shot' by pressing the Print Screen key. This places a copy of the image of the screen on the clipboard.
- Then, with the word processing document open, you can paste this image from the clipboard into the document.

Note: In many instances, whatever has been placed on the clipboard will remain there until you replace it with something else, or close down the system.

CHECK IT YOURSELF

For those intending to complete Unit 6
To be an 'expert user' in the use of software to display data graphically a wide range of techniques and skills are needed. All full-feature software will enable you to produce highly complex and well presented images.

The graphical display checklist given at the end of this chapter includes all the main features you need to be able to use in your particular software. As you progress towards your qualification, complete section 1 of this checklist. Complete section 2 of the checklist on integrating text, data and images and include both sections in your evidence folder as supplementary evidence.

Document transmission by facsimile (fax)

The transmission of exact copies of documents across the telephone network has revolutionised many aspects of the way we work. This means of electronic communication has become a standard way of transmitting key documents. Any document, whether it is handwritten, contains pictures, diagrams, graphs, charts or typed text, can be transmitted at a great speed for relatively low costs (Figure 6.14).

There are many benefits to most organisations in using faxes, including the following:

- Sending a fax is almost instant – you don't need to wait for the next day's mail or the messenger.
- The fax system is widely available – most organisations have at least one fax machine.
- The cost of sending a fax is relatively low compared with, for example, using a messenger.

- International standards have been set which means that you can send faxes to most parts of the world.
- A fax machine can be connected to any telephone socket, so it can be relocated very easily.
- The equipment is very compact and many models are portable.
- You can programme the machine to transmit a fax at a specified time, thus taking advantage of cheaper telephone rates.
- Most fax machines can receive documents automatically, so you don't have to be there when the document is received.
- Many computers have fax capabilities installed in them – you don't even need to print the document but can send the document from the screen or file.

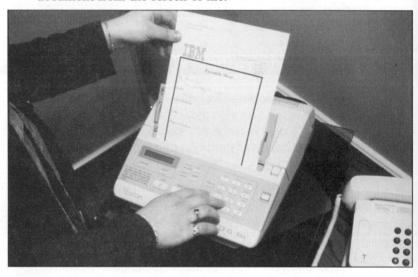

Figure 6.14 A fax machine transmits copies of documents across the telephone network

As with any communications system, good practice can ensure that everything runs smoothly:

- Include a front sheet – you need this to indicate details of who sent the fax and the total number of pages so that the recipient can make sure it has all arrived safely.
- Check the quality of the original documents. Make sure the images are clear and the text is legible – if the original document is not black on white, is damaged or is on the wrong size paper for the machine, it is a good idea to make a photocopy of the original and use the photocopy for the fax transmission.
- Leave a sufficient margin all around as the edges may distort.
- Damaged documents will not easily pass through the machine – make a photocopy and use that.
- Make sure you use the correct size of paper.

- Check the fax number *before* you send the message. The number dialled is usually shown in a display panel – make sure it is correct. If you are sending to a fax/phone number, you will need to make sure that it is set to receive faxes before you transmit, possibly by phoning the recipient to alert him or her to the incoming fax.
- Check received messages to ensure all the pages have transmitted and that they are legible. Call back immediately if the fax needs to be sent again.
- Faxes are usually fairly urgent, so do make sure that in-coming faxes are delivered speedily to the relevant person (see also Chapter 3).

Costs

Faxes are transmitted using telephone lines. The cost of sending a fax is directly related to the length of time it takes to send the fax, the time of day when you send the fax and where you are sending it. If you send a fax of a document that has very little 'white space' – that is, where most of the page has text or graphics on it – it will take longer for the fax to be transmitted and the cost will be greater.

For local transmissions, the costs are often far less than postage rates and, of course, the document will be received much more quickly. When you are sending documents longer distances, the costs are greater than by post but you would weigh this against the time factor to decide which method is more appropriate. International faxing costs need to be considered in terms of the costs compared with the time taken to use the postal system.

Acceptability

Although many organisations are now quite happy to receive orders, contracts, etc., by fax in order to speed up the process of dealing with the information, these copies are still largely unacceptable as legal documents. This means that once you have faxed the document you will also have to send the original by post or courier.

CHECK IT YOURSELF

Do you have access to a fax machine at your workplace? Is there a standard front page for all fax transmissions? How much, on average, does the transmission of a three-page fax cost? Is there a set of guidelines? Place a copy of them in your evidence folder. Enter this information in section 3 of the data communications checklist given at the end of this chapter.

Data transmission

Network communications

Many activities carried out on a day-to-day basis on a computer are only needed in the immediate work environment, but there are many reasons why the computer you work on may be part of a computer network.

Local area networks (LANs) (Figure 6.15) exist where computers are located within relatively short distances of one another, usually within the same building. These are often used so that people within an organisation can share resources such as printers, high-capacity disk storage devices and software, and to enable a range of users to have access to the same data. An electronic mail system can also be established. Similar networks are also frequently set up using telecommunication systems, so that communication and sharing of resources can take place over a wider area (WANs). Many organisations also have links to external networks.

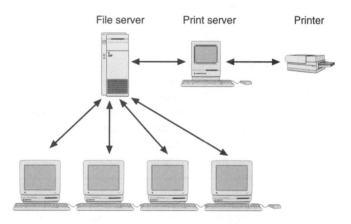

Figure 6.15   Flow of information in a local area network

Electronic mail (e-mail)

Electronic mail, also known as e-mail, is a communications system that enables you to send messages and information with the certainty that it has been placed in the recipient's computer mailbox. E-mail is a way of ensuring rapid, text-based communication both in and outside an organisation. In many organisations, the use of e-mail has replaced the memo and sometimes even letters.

To be able to use e-mail you need to have your computer connected to a network and have the appropriate e-mail software on the system. The mail system, like any other system, has to be managed and supported. There will usually be a post-master who has responsibility for setting up each mailbox, maintaining mailing lists and other network-wide features.

E-mail can improve considerably the internal communications of an organisation, particularly if it is introduced with an appropriate training programme to ensure it is used effectively. However, like all communications systems, it is often used thoughtlessly.

When you are using e-mail you need to be aware of the following:

- E-mail is first read on a computer screen. If the message is too long then it needs to be scrolled up and down, and this can make it much more difficult to take in the detail of the message. Short clear paragraphs are much easier to read on the screen.
- If you are using colours, think of the reader and remember that different screens are set to different levels of contrast and brightness and do not all have the same quality. What looks pleasing and exciting on your screen may not look quite the same to the recipient. It may be too bright, confusing and therefore difficult to read. Have you tried to read red writing on a purple background?
- Read your message before you send it. Does it make sense? Have you missed anything out? We are not all proficient typists, so use the spellcheck to help you correct those slips. You can usually set it up so that this is done automatically before you send the message. Once the 'send' command is pressed it is too late! You can't retrieve an e-mail message unread, as you can a paper message.
- The written word needs to carry all the meaning you intend. There are no other clues, like tone of voice or facial expression, to assist. You need to take care when using capital letters, as they don't always convey the right emphasis. The tone is important. You will probably need to phrase messages to your boss in a different way from those you send to your peer group.
- How many e-mails do you print? E-mail should be reducing the paper flow, but does it increase yours?
- E-mail is only effective if potential users use it. How often do you read your mail?

E-mail lets you not only send and receive mail but also carry out a range of other functions:

- You can send a reply to any message you receive. As the name and e-mail address of the sender are already in the system, you only need to indicate the wish to send a reply and write it, and the system takes care of the rest.
- You can forward any message you have received to any other person within the system.

- You can attach documents and other computer files to your messages. This electronic exchange of files can increase significantly the usefulness of the system.
- Where you need to communicate with a group of people regularly, it is possible to set up a mailing list. Whenever you need to send them messages, you do not need to identify them individually but merely send your message using the mailing list.
- Mailboxes, just like any other mail system, need to be tidied up. You should delete messages that are no longer needed. Messages that need to be kept should be saved in folders, just as you would with a paper system.

E-mail systems operate readily not only across networks within the organisation but also across worldwide networks. Many organisations also provide external e-mail for their employees, usually as part of their links across the Internet. External e-mail has all the features of internal mail and can make a significant difference to business communications.

CHECK IT YOURSELF

What e-mail system do you have access to? Does it operate only within the organisation or are you able to send messages outside the organisation? Is there a post-master within the organisation who is responsible for maintaining the system? Enter this information in section 1 of the data communications checklist.

Electronic noticeboards

E-mail is a means of communicating directly and privately between individuals. However, quite a lot of communication in the workplace is intended for a wide audience. For this type of communication, there is a more effective system, known as electronic noticeboards or bulletin boards.

Under this system, just one copy of the message is placed in a special mailbox which is accessible to all mail users. The message is managed by the person who placed it on the board, and he or she needs to delete it when it is no longer required. By using this system you ensure that no one is left off a mailing list, that only one copy exists within the system rather than a copy in each mailbox, and therefore that copies of the message need not be managed by every user.

Which method of communication would you use for the following tasks? Assume that the recipients will have access to fax and e-mail facilities. Put a ✔ in the box to indicate your choice. If you would follow up by post, put a ✔ in the 'post' box as well.

		Fax	E-mail	Post	Courier
1	A three-page document, of which you have only a printed copy, which needs to be with your customer by first thing next day	☐	☐	☐	☐
2	A highly confidential document that you have word processed and that has to be with your colleague based in another building by this afternoon at the latest	☐	☐	☐	☐
3	A short, urgent letter that you need to know has reached its destination	☐	☐	☐	☐
4	A word processed document with a great deal of scientific formulae. It will need to be returned to you with suggested amendments by tomorrow	☐	☐	☐	☐
5	A poor-quality photocopy of a hand-written eight-page report that needs to be with a colleague at a different office within four days	☐	☐	☐	☐
6	A brief memo to be distributed to every head of department in the organisation	☐	☐	☐	☐
7	The agenda and notice of a planning meeting to be sent to a customer for a meeting scheduled for next Friday	☐	☐	☐	☐
8	Confirmation of an airline booking to be sent to the travel agents	☐	☐	☐	☐
9	A lease that contains plans and needs to be seen first by the client's solicitor and then signed by the client as soon as possible	☐	☐	☐	☐
10	Written details of a very urgent order you want your supplier to start processing this afternoon	☐	☐	☐	☐

Do you have access to an electronic noticeboard? Enter this information in section 2 of the data communications checklist.

Other electronic facilities: electronic diaries and calendars

Electronic diaries and calendars are important features in many electronic offices. In their most sophisticated form it is possible to use them to organise and co-ordinate meetings, the use of facilities such as seminar rooms, and to ensure that everyone is alerted to important dates and times.

 CASE STUDY: Duke's Designs

Figure 6.16 gives details of the diaries of the five people who need to attend a meeting some time this week, and also gives the bookings for the meeting room. The meeting is expected to last at least one and a half hours. Can you suggest two possible times for this meeting?

Suzie's diary

MONDAY 9.30-12.00 Review meeting 3.15-4.00 Mike & Tom	THURSDAY 12.30-2.00 Lunch with Anna
TUESDAY	FRIDAY 10.15-11.30 Printers
WEDNESDAY 4.15-? Computer group	Notes 4.15 Train on Friday to Dover

Anna's diary

MONDAY ALL DAY Central London meeting	THURSDAY 12.30-2.00 Lunch with Suzie 2.00-4.30 Amrita (P&D)
TUESDAY 8.45-9.30 Design group 12.00-1.30 Lunch - Art team	FRIDAY
WEDNESDAY 3.30 Bank Manager	Notes Logo design Crink & Totem by end of the week

Nadeem's diary

MONDAY	THURSDAY 3.30 Elites - Coventry
TUESDAY	FRIDAY 1 day LEAVE
WEDNESDAY 9.15-10.45 Review with Jan 4.15-? Computer group	Notes Not back until Monday pm

Mike's diary

MONDAY 3.15-4.00 Suzie & Tom	THURSDAY
TUESDAY 4.30-5.00 Ade (artwork)	FRIDAY
WEDNESDAY 4.15 Computer group	Notes

Jaya's diary		Meeting room bookings	
MONDAY	THURSDAY 12.00-12.45 New photocopier	MONDAY 4.30 Committee meeting	THURSDAY
TUESDAY 2.00-3.15 Review meeting	FRIDAY 9.00-12.30 Wells – new brief	TUESDAY 8.45-9.30 Design group	FRIDAY EXTERNAL BOOKING ALL DAY
WEDNESDAY	Notes	WEDNESDAY 3.30 Training session	Notes Need OHP for Wednesday & Friday

Figure 6.16 Diaries

How long did this task take you? It would have been so much quicker to co-ordinate these details in an electronic diary, which would have automatically selected the best time. The system could also have been used to notify everyone concerned of the final arrangements!

It is important to be aware, however, that this type of system is only effective if *everyone* keeps his or her diary up to date. Supposing Anna had forgotten to enter a three-hour health and safety course that was booked for 9.00 am on Thursday – what difference would this have made?

CHECK IT YOURSELF

Do you have access to electronic diaries and calendars? Enter this information in section 2 of the data communications checklist.

External networks

Whatever kind of work you do and regardless of the type of organisation you work in, there is a need to communicate both inside and outside the organisation. The way this is done is changing rapidly with the growth of worldwide networks and the ever-reducing costs of both the hardware and the communications software necessary to achieve this.

The Internet

The Internet has been around for a long time, but until fairly recently was primarily used by the US military (DARPA) and the higher education sector (JANET). However, since the early 1990s its use has grown extremely rapidly both for home and business users. In very simple terms, it is a group of networks that use the same *protocol* (set of rules) to communicate.

To connect to the Internet you will usually have access via an Internet Provider (IP) and the system must be using the standard rules and procedures for connecting – TCP/IP (transmission control protocol/Internet protocol). If you are a home user or in a very small organisation you may be connecting via a modem, a device for converting analogue signals to digital signals and back again (**mo**dulator/**dem**odulator). However, many businesses will be linking through a dedicated network line to the service provider.

There are various aspects of the Internet; the one that you are most likely to use is the World Wide Web (WWW). This is a graphical user interface (GUI) to access the resources on the Internet. What this means in simple terms is that it is 'user-friendly' and works with pictures and interactive multimedia techniques. Using HTML (hypertext mark-up language), pages are linked to enable the user to 'surf' the net. By clicking on hyperlinks, the user links to other pages all around the network. These links may lead to text, images, video clips, sounds and a wide range of services.

To be able to access the World Wide Web you need to have a browser. This is software that can read the HTML files. The web browser will enable you to navigate the web (move around the pages), to down-load images and text, and to print.

The information on the Internet is not organised, nor is it controlled or managed in any way. This means you need some assistance if you are to find what you are looking for. To be able to search effectively across this network of information you will often need to use one of the many *search engines* that are available. These are interactive services with access to vast catalogues of hundreds of thousands of web sites which can be found through key word searches. There is an ever-increasing number of the tools available and some of the more sophisticated ones 'learn' about responses to searches so that they can improve their search results.

For many businesses, the primary use of the Internet is the provision of worldwide e-mail facilities. They have yet to appreciate its full capabilities or the impact that it may have on the way they conduct their business. For some, the Internet has the potential to provide opportunities for telling the rest of the world about their organisation and its products and services; it could be a wonderful marketing medium. For other organisations it can provide, through the use of FTP (file transfer protocol), a means of transmitting data around the world.

CHECK IT YOURSELF

Do you have access to the Internet where you work? Find out the name of the provider and how the connection is made (dial-up or dedicated link).

What type of activities does the organisation use the Internet for? Is there a set of guidelines on using the Internet? Place a copy of them in your evidence folder. Enter this information in section 4 of the data communications checklist.

External databases

Many databases are available for reference purposes, and are not related to a specific area of business but can improve the efficiency of an organisation. The Internet can provide access to many of these, although access to some may also be limited or restricted to subscribers or members of a closed user group.

Not all remote databases are linked to the Internet, however. For many businesses, there are remote (external) databases which they need to access for their daily operations. The travel business needs access to airline bookings systems; for stock exchanges around the world, dealing takes place via access to online computerised databases; spare parts for cars are ordered through direct links to manufacturers' databases. These are examples of *interactive* databases. Others are designed for reference only, such as Mediline.

Many of these uses are for closed user groups. The data is *not* available to the general public, nor is it free, but only available to paying subscribers. These types of links are usually connected using dial-up telephone links via a modem, dedicated telephone lines known as a megastream where the link is permanently established or, where the links need to be of particularly high speeds, but only of short duration, by a (relatively expensive) ISDN line.

CHECK IT YOURSELF

Do you have access to any external databases? How are they provided: through dial-up, megastream links or ISDN, or some other connection? What type of information is available and what do you use it for? Enter this information in section 5 of the data communications checklist.

Videoconferencing

A relatively new and exciting development that could significantly change the way many people work is videoconferencing. One of the major concerns about the changing way of working, with an ever-increasing emphasis on the use of new technologies, is the reduction in opportunities for interaction between people.

Videoconferencing became popular during the Gulf war when many business people did not want to travel for fear of hijack or sabotage. It used to mean (and for some, still does) going to a special studio and using TV technology. Now, with videoconferencing equipment and communications links becoming more sophisticated, cheaper, and therefore more accessible, this is changing.

Each participant in a videoconference will need the following:

- A device to 'capture' video (a digital video camera).
- A microphone – although a conference can take place by 'talking' through the keyboard.
- Speakers – assuming you are using voice contact.
- A computer – capable of handling the digitised video input.
- Software to 'manage' the conference.
- A communication channel – this could be ISDN or cable or across the Internet.

There are three ways a conference can take place. *Point-to-point* (see Figure 6.17) is the simplest form of conference. One Internet user calls another. You need to know the IP (Internet provider) address of the other person.

Figure 6.17 Point-to-point videoconferencing

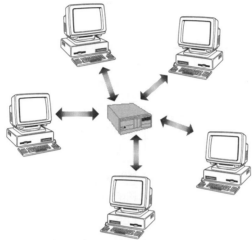

Figure 6.18 A group videoconference

In a *group* conference (Figure 6.18), a number of users simultaneously contact a central computer which is running *reflector* software. You need to know the IP address of the reflector site. A *broadcast* conference (Figure 6.19) is similar to a group conference, except the flow of communication is one way only. The reflector site is used to transmit information to any connected user.

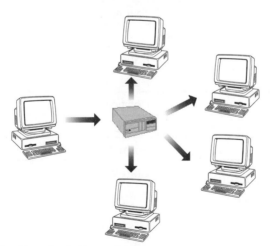

Figure 6.19 A broadcast videoconference

Text processing checklist

Section 1: formatting functions

Appearance	Different fonts	☐
	Size of text	☐
	Bold	☐
	Italics	☐
	Underlining	☐
	Other	☐
Margins	Left and right	☐
	Top and bottom	☐
	Header and footer	☐
Indent	Left and right	☐
	Hanging	☐
	First line	☐
Tabs	Left	☐
	Right	☐
	Centre	☐
	Decimal	☐
	Leaders	☐
Paragraphs	Justification	☐
	Line spacing	☐
	Text flow	

Section 2: document layout

Page layout	Page size	☐
	Page orientation	☐
Page numbering	Positioning	☐
	First page	☐
	Format	☐
	Start value	☐

Text processing checklist (continued)

Headers and footers	First page	☐
	Alternate page	☐
	New sections	☐
	Footnotes	☐
Columns	Newspaper	☐
	Parallel	☐
Presentation	Lines	☐
	Boxes	☐

Section 3: document structure

Directories	Indexing	☐
	Table of contents	☐
Paragraph numbering	Numbers	☐
	Bullets	☐
	Multilevel	☐

Section 4: other

Data checking	Spellcheck	☐
	Thesaurus	☐
	Print preview	☐
Document handling	Merge	☐
	Sort	☐

Graphical images checklist

Section 1: image creation

Image types	Bitmap (new)	☐
	Bitmap (amend)	☐
	Vector (new)	☐
	Vector (amend)	☐
Input devices	Keyboard	☐
	Mouse	☐
	Scanner	☐
	Digitiser	☐
	Other	☐
Output	Greyscale	☐
	Colour	☐
	Transparencies	☐
	Other	☐

Section 2: image attributes

Colour	Predefined	☐
	Define own	☐
	Effects	☐
Patterns	Predefined	☐
	Define own	☐
Form	Size	☐
	Shape	☐

Section 3: image presentation

Layout	Size	☐
	Orientation	☐
Manipulation	Rotation	☐
	Scaling	☐
	Inversion	☐

Graphical images checklist (continued)

Section 4: elements

Line	Type	☐
	Thickness	☐
Shape	Predefined	☐
	Define own	☐
	Objects	☐
Text	Different fonts	☐
	Size of text	☐
	Bold	☐
	Italics	☐

Data modelling checklist

Section 1: model layout

Page layout	Page size	☐
	Page orientation	☐
Page numbering	Positioning	☐
	Format	☐
Headers and footers	Date	☐
	Time	☐
	Filename	☐
Size	Columns	☐
	Rows	☐

Section 2: model formatting

Cell formats	Text	☐
	Numeric	
	integer	☐
	decimal	☐
	currency	☐
	Date	☐
Appearance	Different fonts	☐
	Size of text	☐
	Bold	☐
	Italics	☐
	Other	☐
Margins	Left and right	☐
	Top and bottom	☐
	Header and footer	☐

Data modelling checklist (continued)

Section 3: manipulating models

Arithmetic calculations	Add	☐
	Subtract	☐
	Multiply	☐
	Divide	☐
	Cell reference	
	relative	☐
	absolute	☐
Functions	Sum	☐
	Average	☐
	Percentage	☐
Conditional functions	Logical	☐
	Arithmetic	☐

Graphical display checklist

Graphical display of data

Section 1: Type of display		
	Pie chart	☐
	Line graph	☐
	Bar chart	☐
Control display	Positioning	☐
	Axis scale	☐
Annotation	Labels	☐
	Legends	☐
	Titles	☐

Section 2: Integration of software		
Into text-based documents	Images	☐
	Numerical models	☐
	Graphical displays	☐
	Structured data	☐
	Text	☐
	Other	☐
Into numerical models	Text	☐
	Graphical displays	☐
	Other	☐

Data communications checklist

Section 1: e-mail

Name of e-mail system	
Is this an internal *only* system?	Yes/No
If there is an external system, who is the provider?	
Who is the post-master?	
Network software	
Version number	

Section 2

Do you have electronic noticeboards?	Yes/No
Do you use an electronic diary or calendar?	Yes/No

Section 3: fax

Is there a standard front page?	Yes/No
What is the average cost of a three-page fax?	
Do you have a set of guidelines?	Yes/No

Section 4: Internet

Do you have access to the Internet?	Yes/No
Name of the Internet provider	
Method of connection	Dial-up ☐ Dedicated link ☐
What type of activities is it used for?	
Do you have a set of guidelines?	Yes/No

Section 5: external databases

Do you have access to an external database?	Yes/No
How are connections made?	
What type of data is held?	
What do you use it for?	

7 Enhancing ways of working

When you have gained your qualification, you will be well on the way to becoming an 'expert user'. As you progress towards this award, you will become increasingly aware of the range of skills and knowledge this implies. Your colleagues and employers will expect you to be able to advise and recommend better ways of using the existing facilities as well as improvements or enhancements that could be made to the software and hardware.

To be able to do this effectively you need to be confident in the skills you have, aware of the limitations of your knowledge and therefore when and where to seek support or assistance, adventurous in your use of the computer systems and determined that your skills and knowledge will stay current (up to date). In the world of technology, you can't stand still for too long!

Personal development

What computers are used for and the ways they are used are constantly changing. This means that most people who use computers in their work need to be continuously updating their skills just to stay in the same place. Every few months there seems to be yet another release of the software you use, a bigger, faster processor, etc., and of course with this comes the need to relearn the skills you already have. Yet ideally what you should be trying to do is *increase* your skills level rather than just staying still.

Figure 7.1 Keeping up to date with computer skills can feel like running hard to keep still

In many organisations, the main responsibility for ensuring that staff skills are current rests in the first instance with the employees. Most managers don't like their staff to come to them with problems but with *solutions* to problems. When it comes to training and retraining they want to know what skills you need and how you intend to get them!

What you need to do is consider the following:

- How do you ensure your skills are current?
- Are there training opportunities available to you through your workplace?
- Where would you like to be in a year's time?

CHECK IT YOURSELF

It is probably a good idea for you to draw up a development plan for yourself. You may well be able to use this as the basis for negotiations in discussions with your supervisor or your tutor. What should you include in this plan? A current skills analysis is usually a good place to start – try to do this against the tasks identified in your job description.

Current skills analysis

1 List the things you do regularly and do effectively.
2 List the things you think you could do better if you had additional training.
3 List the things you need to be able to do but don't yet have the skills for.
4 List the things you would like to be able to do but don't yet have the skills for.
5 Identify how each of these would benefit the organisation.
6 Identify how each of these would benefit you and your future.
7 Identify which of these you could 'explore' and start to learn for yourself.
8 Identify which of these would require some training.

You now need to prioritise this list:

1 Put in order of greatest need those in points (2) and (3) above.
2 Put in order of most likely benefit to the organisation those in point (4).
3 Choose one that you could 'explore' and one in which you need training from each of these new lists.
4 Put all this information into a simple report for your supervisor/tutor.

You now need to take this forward with your supervisor or tutor. Arrange an appointment with your supervisor/tutor to discuss it (supply a copy of the report *before* the meeting so that your supervisor has had time to consider what you are proposing).

One way to help you identify the skills you have, and the further skills you need to acquire, is to look at job advertisements. This will often help you to set goals for the future and to decide which skills and personal training might help you achieve them.

CHECK IT YOURSELF

In the appendix **Applying for a job**, on page 170, there are five job advertisements. Read through them and choose one that you might be interested in working towards, even if you do not have the necessary skills and experience at the moment.

What additional training would you need to prepare yourself for this job? Make a list. How might you acquire these skills? Are there courses at your local college? What books might be of use? Is it possible for you to get training in the workplace?

Professional development: finding your way around

Using a computer system in a working environment should normally enable you to work more efficiently and effectively. If the task you have to do is more time consuming on the computer or does not produce better results than a manual system, then you are probably not making full use of the system's capabilities.

As you become more experienced with the system, you will be able to develop techniques and skills on your own. The hardware and software now available have many features that will assist you with this. Often the best way to find out about these is to explore. Software is usually provided with a set of manuals which detail how all the different parts of the software work. Most software will also have some form of online help facility, and this can be a good starting point for your exploration. There are few systems today that can be damaged by exploring in this way.

In addition, many software packages are supplied with an online tutorial which will take you through some of these procedures step by step. If you are not sure what you are doing you should seek advice from your supervisor or tutor or refer to a manual.

Select one software package you know fairly well and use for a variety of tasks. Do you have access to a supplier's reference manual? Have you been provided with other written information on how to use it? Does it have an online help facility? Do you have an online tutorial for this software? Enter these details on the enhancements checklist given at the end of this chapter.

Reference manuals

Suppliers' reference manuals are often technical and not always very easy to use. However, you need to become used to them as there may be occasions when you will need to refer to them.

For most users, the manual you will need to refer to is the *User's Guide*. This will usually cater for both the completely new user and also the experienced person who needs to dip in as necessary. Many of these manuals adopt a similar format, and you can reasonably expect to find the following features in most:

- *Contents*   The contents lists the main headings and subheadings for each section of the manual. This list is in sequential order and will include page numbers.
- *Getting started*   This will explain, step by step, how to start to use the software. It will usually include information on how to install it, load it and exit from it, together with a guide on the start-up features and possibly an overview of the package.
- *Basic features*   This section will usually have precise details about how to use the general and most widely used features of the package. This information may be presented in alphabetical order of commands or may be as groups of commands that cover an aspect of the package. For new users this is the section they are likely to refer to most often during the early stages.
- *Advanced features*   The section on advanced features will contain details of the more complex aspects of the software. The presentation will usually follow the same format as that used for the basic features. This section may never be referred to by many users, but if you are going to become an 'expert user' you should familiarise yourself with what is included in this section even if you do not need detailed experience of using these commands.
- *Customising*   In this section you will find details of how to change the way the package works to suit the way you wish to work. It may also include information on how to alter the setup to match your particular configuration.
- *Appendix*   There may be a number of appendices which will usually contain technical specifications, etc.
- *Glossary*   The glossary will contain definitions of technical terms and words used in a particular way specific to the package.

- *Index* The index is an alphabetical list with section and page references. For most 'expert users' this is the starting point if they wish to find something in the manual.

There is also a wide range of commercially produced books and quick reference guides for the more commonly used software packages. These are very useful for those who know how to use the software but need something to refer to, particularly for commands they do not use very often.

CHECK IT YOURSELF

If possible, obtain a copy of a supplier's manual for one of the pieces of software you know fairly well. Using the index, find the information on how to carry out two or three features you *do* know how to use. Read these and compare with your own understanding of these features.

Now select something you *do not* know about. You could do this by reference to the contents or the index. Read it through and then try it out on the computer. Try to think of a particular use you might have for this new feature. How 'user-friendly' is the manual? Record this on the enhancements checklist.

Online help

Much of the information contained in a supplier's manual will also be available in a good online help facility. One of the main advantages of

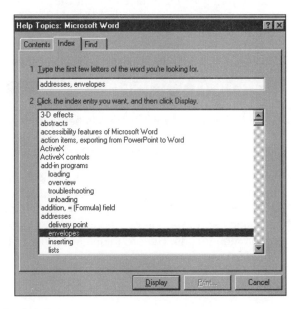

Figure 7.2 Online help index

using the online help system is that you can call it up on to your screen as and when you need it. However, a word of warning: not all these systems are very helpful and none of them contains every detail about the software.

CHECK IT YOURSELF

Now repeat the last activity, but this time using the online help. You will usually be able to look things up in a similar way by referring to the contents or search index. Is the same information provided, and to the same level of explanation? Is the online help 'user-friendly'? Record this on the enhancements checklist.

Customising setups

When software is installed it is usually put on to the system with the default setups as supplied by the manufacturer. However, this is often not the particular way in which you or your organisation wishes to use the package. The software will need to be set to get the best from your particular hardware in terms of use of memory, type of printing facilities and most frequently used aspects of the package. Most organisations will want to have a level of standardisation in terms of printed output to present a corporate image (see also Chapter 5).

Many organisations will require that all their users have the same setup for ease of maintenance and upgrading, whilst some aspects of the desk top may be customised to suit the individual user. For most people there is an optimum colour scheme which causes least stress and may even improve productivity.

CHECK IT YOURSELF

Who decides how your system is set up? Has the software been customised to meet the needs of the organisation, or has it been installed with the default settings?

Identify two aspects of the way one particular package has been set up that could be changed to improve your efficiency. Do you have the authority to make these changes? If not, find out who makes these decisions and what the procedure is for you to put forward your recommendations. Record this in section 2 of the enhancements checklist.

Automation of functions

For most computer users, many of their tasks are done on a regular basis. Whether it is extracting sets of information from a database or typing a memo, many aspects of the activity are the same. It therefore makes sense to find ways of reducing the repetition and of getting the computer to assist you in your work. It is often relatively simple to automate or semi-automate these tasks using some of the more advanced features of the software package.

Most desktop software used today will have a feature called a *macro*. Macros are small routines which can be predefined to carry out a sequence of instructions or events within the software. Once they have been defined they can be run, or executed, whenever required. These macros may be very small, simple routines or may be quite complex and interactive with the user – for example, to complete a standard form.

Are any of the functions you carry out automated? Do you have the authority to define your automatic functions? Is there a procedure in the organisation to set them up? Think about the activities you carry out on a regular basis. Identify one aspect of one of the packages you use that could benefit from automation. Enter these details in section 3 of the enhancements checklist.

Write a proposal for your supervisor/tutor suggesting that you carry out this improvement. It will need to include the following:

1 Description of the task.
2 Details of how it could be improved. This could involve
 • speed of production;
 • improved accuracy of the data;
 • improved quality of presentation; and
 • reduction in technical expertise required.
3 Details of the resources necessary to make this change (if any).
4 Implications for the users (changes in the way they work).
5 Implications for others (e.g. change in the version of the software).
6 Timescale to implement (include a retraining programme if appropriate).

Enhancements checklist

Section 1: reference material

Name of software package	
Supplier's reference manual?	Yes/No
Is the manual 'user-friendly'?	Yes/No
Written user instructions?	Yes/No
Online help facility?	Yes/No
Is the online help 'user-friendly'?	Yes/No
Online tutorial?	Yes/No

Section 2: customising

Has the software been customised?	Yes/No
Do you have the authority to make any changes?	Yes/No
If not, who does?	
Is there a procedure to propose changes?	Yes/No
What changes would you propose?	

1

2

Section 3: automation

Are there any automated functions?	Yes/No
Do you have the authority to define your own?	Yes/No
If not, who does?	
Is there a procedure to propose and record them?	Yes/No

What automation would you propose?

8 Working within the legislation

The use of computers in all areas of work and leisure is growing rapidly. As a computer user, you need to know about the various aspects of legislation relating to working with computers. The main areas you need to be particularly aware of are data protection, copyright issues and computer misuse. You also need to know about the health and safety requirements. This is covered in detail in Chapter 9.

Data protection

What is meant by data protection and why is it necessary? More and more information about people is being stored on computers and more and more people have easier access to it:

- Worldwide communication systems are becoming more powerful by the day. It is now possible for data held almost anywhere in the world to be accessed rapidly in most other parts of the world.
- The speed and processing powers of computers mean that facts and figures about individuals are more likely to be analysed and brought together.
- The proliferation of computers in both business and the home means that almost anyone has access to this technology. As the cost of online access is reducing rapidly, so this expansion will undoubtedly continue.

There are many advantages to this widespread computerised data access, but it brings with it the need to ensure that the data, and the individuals concerned, are protected. How many organisations do you think hold data about you in an electronic form?

Figure 8.1 gives a list of likely computerised record holders for most people in the UK today. The list is by no means complete, but is intended to highlight the extent of electronic collection and storage of personal data. Most of the time we are not made aware that this information is going to be held as a permanent record and we rarely think twice about supplying the details. Although data users are required to advise you that this information about you will be held, and to give you the opportunity to request that they do not make it available elsewhere, this notification is often in such small print that you don't notice it.

Whilst most users record this data for entirely legitimate reasons, there are many organisations who 'sell on' mailing lists which frequently result in junk mail and unsolicited sales approaches.

Go through the list in Figure 8.1 and decide how many of these data users probably have data about you. Are there any others you can think of? Add them to the list.

Organisation	Type of data	Tick the ones that apply to you
Health authority	Personal details including name of doctor	
Doctor	Medical history	
Local authority	Residential and possibly employment and benefit details	
Bank	Credit rating and history, some employment details	
Employer	Employment history, some medical records	
DVLC Swansea	Car and driving licence details	
PNC	Car details	
Inland Revenue	Tax and employment history	
Education authority	Education and some family details	
Insurance companies	Motor – motoring offences, driving details and history; Life – health, employment, family details; Home – home security, value of possessions	
Credit card and hire-purchase companies	Credit rating, income, expenditure, lifestyle	
Societies and organisations, e.g. AA, RAC, Reader's Digest, etc.	Limited but tend to have lifestyle details	
Large retail outlets where you have used a credit card	Basic personal details plus details of purchasing history	

Figure 8.1 Computerised record holders

What is the legislation?

The legislation that needs to be considered includes both (a) that which relates specifically to this country and is usually made by the passing of an Act of Parliament; and (b) the requirements of the European Union, which are usually set down as directives to which all member countries must then conform. The current British legislation is the Data Protection Act 1984. This Act relates only to personal data held in an electronic form about living people. It is based on eight guiding principles:

- Data must be obtained legally and fairly.
- Data must be held only for specified purposes – these have to be identified at registration.
- Data must not be used for purposes other than those specified.
- Data must be adequate, relevant and not excessive – the amount of data held should be the minimum necessary to meet the specified purposes.
- Data must be accurate and kept up to date.
- Data must not be held for longer than is necessary.
- Data subjects should be able to access their data and, where appropriate, have it corrected or deleted.
- Security systems must exist to ensure that unauthorised users cannot access, alter, destroy or disclose data.

How does it work?

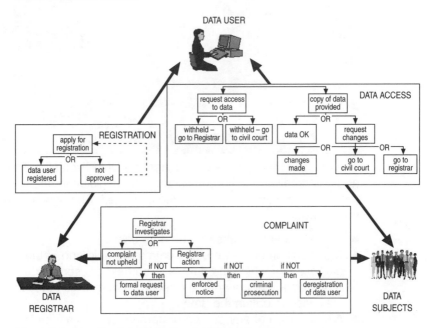

Figure 8.2 How the Data Protection Act 1984 operates

The main operational aspects of this Act (see Figure 8.2) are the requirements on all data users (the people and organisations who hold the data) to

1 register details of the types of data they hold and for what purposes;
2 ensure that their systems have adequate controls to maintain the integrity of the data;
3 ensure that they have adequate security on their systems to safeguard against unauthorised access; and
4 set up procedures to enable data subjects to access their data and to have corrected any inaccuracies, unnecessary records or misuse.

CASE STUDY: The Laitwood Medical Centre

The doctors in this well established practice have recently had installed a small network of computers to run their patient record and administration system so that they can be more responsive to the needs of their patients.

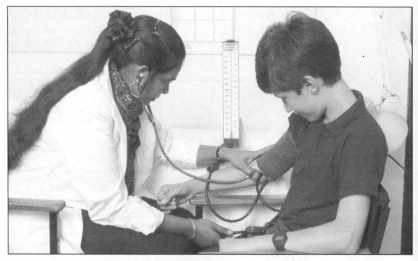

The practice manager has contacted the Data Protection Registrar and has received all the details about the legislation, the forms to register as a data user and the fees charged. She now has to supply the following:

- The name and address of the data user.
- A description of the personal data to be held and of the purpose or purposes for which the data is to be held or used.
- A description of the source or sources from which they intend or may wish to obtain the data.
- A description of any person or persons to whom they intend or may wish to disclose the data.

- The names or a description of any countries or territories outside the UK to which they intend or may wish directly or indirectly to transfer the data.
- One or more addresses for the receipt of requests from data subjects for access to the data.

Using this information, carry out the following tasks:

1 Create a table with three columns. In the first column, make a list of all the items of personal data you think the practice might want to keep on its computer system.
2 In the second column, enter the sources of each item of data, i.e. who will supply the data.
3 In the third column, enter against each data item the people or organisations to whom the data may be disclosed.

Discuss what you have put into this table with your tutor.

The Data Protection Register, which contains the details supplied by data users, is a public document. A copy should be available in major public libraries.

CHECK IT YOURSELF

In most organisations there will be a person who is responsible for all matters connected with this legislation. Find out the name and job title of the person who has this responsibility in your organisation. Enter this information in section 1 of the legislation checklist given at the end of this chapter. You may also be able to get a copy of the details of the organisation's registration. If you can, include this in your portfolio of evidence.

Having identified and registered details of the personal data that are to be held, the data user then needs to make sure that systems are set up to ensure the quality, accuracy and integrity of the data (see Chapter 5).

CHECK IT YOURSELF

What controls exist on the systems you work on? Find at least two examples for all three aspects of data integrity identified in Chapter 5 and enter the information on the legislation checklist.

Are there procedures in your organisation for handling breaches or potential breaches of security? To whom would you report your concerns, and how? Are there any instances you might have authority to deal with, and what would you do? Write a brief description and draft a memo to report this to the appropriate authority. Include this in your evidence folder.

CASE STUDY: The Laitwood Medical Centre

The practice manager is very aware of the need to ensure that only authorised personnel have access to patient records. Also, particularly as the centre is open to large numbers of members of the public, good security systems must be in place to make sure that confidentiality of the data is maintained.

There is a computer in each of the consulting rooms so that the doctors have access to the patients' files during each appointment. As these rooms are usually locked when not in use, these do not pose much of a security risk in terms of unauthorised access.

There are two computers in the general office, on the ground floor of the building. These are used by a number of staff including the practice nurse, the administration assistant and the practice manager and, occasionally, by one of the doctors.

In the reception area there is one computer, which is mainly used for booking appointments, although sometimes other staff within the practice may use it, particularly outside surgery hours:

1   What general security procedures do you think the practice manager needs to put in place throughout the practice?
2   What are the particular concerns regarding:
    ● the positioning of the equipment in the reception area; and
    ● the different access levels of computers in the general office?

Discuss your answers with your tutor.

The legislation is designed to stop the storage of 'unnecessary' personal data. No data user should be holding personal data without good reason, nor should data be kept for longer than necessary. When data users register, they are required to specify the purpose for which they are holding the data. As a data subject you may challenge this and have the data deleted if you can demonstrate that there is no legitimate reason for keeping it, but first you need to be able to see exactly what is held.

The data subjects – the people that the data relates to – can request access to most data to check that the information is accurate and held for legitimate purposes. All registered data users are required to have a procedure for data subjects to gain access to their data.

CASE STUDY: The Laitwood Medical Centre

The practice manager needs to set up the procedure for data subjects to request access to their data. The Data Protection Act specifies the following:

- The organisation can charge a fee for providing the access. It is currently set at a *maximum* of £10 for each category of registration.
- The request for access needs to be in writing.
- The organisation must obtain satisfactory proof of identity before disclosing any details.
- The data must be supplied, once all the above have been met, within 40 days.

The practice manager has decided that a leaflet is needed to explain the procedure. Assuming that the practice provides a form for people to fill in to make their request, produce a simple, clear leaflet to tell people what information they can find out and how to do this.

CHECK IT YOURSELF

What are the procedures in the organisation where you are working? Is there a standard form to complete? Ask for a copy of it to keep in your portfolio. Does the organisation charge an administration fee, and if so how much? Enter this information in section 1 of the legislation checklist.

Breaches of the data protection legislation

What should you do if you become aware of a breach in the legislation? First, you need to make sure that you are familiar with the procedures within your organisation for dealing with this situation. Although you are fully aware of the requirements of the law, your colleagues and supervisor may not know the details. As the 'expert', and a responsible employee, you should advise them of the situation whenever necessary. This should be done as tactfully as possible, drawing their attention to the organisation's procedures for ensuring compliance with the legislation and dealing with any breaches.

The most recent development in legislation in the EU is the 1995 European Directive on Protection of Personal Data. This aims to minimise the differences between national protection laws throughout the EU to make free movement of personal data possible within the EU. Within three years, member states will have incorporated this into their legislation.

The main benefits of this will be as follows:

- Any person whose data is processed in the EU will have equal protection of his or her rights, in particular the right to privacy, regardless of which member state the processing is being carried out in.

- The directive is intended to prevent the EU rules being avoided where data is being transferred to a non-EU country.
- For non-EU countries where adequate protection is provided, the free flow of data from all EU states will be assured.

Copyright

Copyright is about the ownership of rights in printed and recorded materials and software. It restricts what you are allowed to copy, how many times and for what purposes. The contents of this book are covered by copyright law. The author and publisher had to make sure that the words and images used did not 'belong' to anyone else. The copyright of this book belongs to the author. If you wish to use something that belongs to someone else, you must seek permission, acknowledge the copyright and, usually, pay to be allowed to use it. If you don't, it is the same as stealing.

Figure 8.3 Breaking copyright rules is the same as stealing

There are two different areas of concern regarding copyright and IT. One relates to software and the conditions under which you are permitted to use it, and the other is about the use of data, images and text which are held in digital form.

Software

Software is very costly to produce and very easy to copy. When you acquire an item of software you do not usually own the software – what you have purchased is a licence to use it. There are many different types of licences and it is always important to read the small print to make sure you are aware of what you can and cannot do. The licence could be any one of the following:

- *Single-user licence*   You may use this software on one computer only – the licence is usually for the user, who may transfer the software from one machine to another as long as it can be used on only one machine at any time.
- *Multiuser licence*   You may have an agreed number of users with access to this software – this may be by installation on a set number of computers, or it could be for specified numbers with network access.
- *Site licence*   You may be licensed to use the software for all the users on a site – some software providers consider a site to mean a physical location, whilst others can interpret it more loosely and it could mean a whole organisation.
- *Machine licence*   Sometimes the software licence is attached to a particular computer rather than the user – in this instance you cannot transfer the software to a different computer without the permission of the copyright holder.
- *Server licence*   On a network, the licence may be restricted, like a machine licence, to a particular network server.
- *Network licence*   In a network environment you may have a licence for software to be used across the whole network – again there are a number of different ways the term network is interpreted. Most network systems software will be licensed under a network licence.

CHECK IT YOURSELF

Who is responsible for ensuring that adequate licences exist for the software you work with? What is his or her job title? Is there a central record of software licences? If so, where is it held? Enter these details in section 2 of the legislation checklist.

It is illegal to copy and use software in a way that has not been licensed. It is extremely unlikely that anyone working in an IT department would ask you to do this. It is possible, however, that someone who doesn't understand copyright law could ask you; for example, a person who has some software on a computer at home and would like to use it at work. If this happens, you should politely explain the law and consult your supervisor.

Some software is provided on a different basis, such as shareware and freeware. This is often software that has not been developed by a commercial organisation and therefore there is not the same concern about loss of income through unauthorised copying.

Shareware software is usually freely distributed in an unsupported form. It will come with details of how you can pay a nominal charge which will entitle you to patches (corrections), add-ons (enhanced features) and updates.

Freeware is software for which there is no charge, and can be freely distributed and used. This sort of software is not usually a full-feature application but often consists of a number of utilities and useful routines. This may be distributed through CD-ROMs attached to magazines, etc., or could be available on the Internet.

Data, images and text

In recent years the development of technologies that enable data, images and text to be readily captured and held in digital form has considerably increased concern about copyright. All the aspects of copyright in the print world now also apply in the digital world, but are more complex and potentially more difficult to control.

One of the most notable recent developments is the availability of scanners and software which not only capture images and store them electronically but also have the capability to convert scanned text pages into text characters that can be manipulated through word processors, etc. This means that large quantities of words can be rapidly stored, altered and transmitted across networks. It also means that in the course of your everyday work, it would be easy to reproduce text and images belonging to someone else, without considering the fact that you are breaching copyright regulations.

Computer misuse

A whole range of activities can be considered under the term misuse. Many organisations are reluctant to report or publicise the extent to which some of these activities take place because of the damage it could do to their credibility.

Breaking in

The act of breaking in to a computer system (hacking) is in itself a crime. It is also the first stage of doing damage to the system. Employees' carelessness with passwords is a common cause of unauthorised access. Also, particularly in a system where there are a great many users and passwords, hackers can find out passwords by trial and error. Too many people choose 'obvious' character combinations for their passwords, such as date of birth, the name of a friend or member of the family. To skilled and determined hackers these are their first choices when attempting a break in.

Altering data

Once inside the computer system the hacker, or other unauthorised user, may gain access to sensitive data. Employees and others from outside the organisation may alter data for their own benefit. Changes may be made to an employee's payroll data so that he or she is 'overpaid'; accounts receivable entries may be wiped out so that a customer is not charged for goods received; or accounts and charges in an accounts payable system may be set up so that customers are charged (and possibly pay) for goods or services they never receive. Finally there is the possibility of wilful destruction of an entire database; this can be guarded against by the operation of regular and comprehensive backup procedures.

Theft of data and espionage

With the increasing use of computers for design purposes, many product plans may be vulnerable to theft through unauthorised access by competitors. Valuable customer details and company 'secrets' can be stolen and sold to competitors for profit.

Altering programs

Sometimes a minor change to a program can enable someone to profit fraudulently. There have been a number of examples where employees have transferred the 'rounded down' fractions of amounts of money to their own or fictitious accounts and have succeeded, over several years, in committing significant thefts.

Theft of computer time

Many people use their access to their employer's computers to carry out their own activities. It is not at all uncommon for employees to word process the occasional personal letter, or to prepare their CVs to help them apply for new jobs. These activities are rarely considered to be a major problem although they are still a misuse of the computer system. However, there are many instances of employees using their employers' computer system to carry out activities for which they are being paid by others. In many organisations this would be treated as a disciplinary offence for which you could be sacked.

What can organisations do to combat these activities?

Most organisations will have some level of security for access to the buildings, the staff work areas (particularly if it is a place that is open to the general public), and the computer systems (mainly through passwords, location of equipment, etc.). However, much of this crime is brought about through failure to follow procedures. How easy is it to 'talk your way in' to the building where you work or study, or walk in unchallenged? How secure are your passwords (see Chapter 5)? What procedures exist for handling confidential information? What should you do if you become aware of breaches of security or misuse?

CHECK IT YOURSELF

Produce a brief, word processed report on the security systems in your organisation (this could be where you work, or at college). This will need to include information about getting into the building as an employee/student, arrangements for visitors, and areas open to the general public. Describe the procedures for access to the computer systems, both physical security and passwords. If possible, include an example of a breach of security and how it was dealt with.

Legislation checklist

Section 1: data protection

Name of person with responsibility	
Job title	
Is there a standard form?	Yes/No
Administration fee?	£
Systems to ensure integrity of data	

1 Checks at data entry

2 Controls during processing

3 Control of access

Section 2: copyright

Name of person with responsibility	
Job title	
Is there a central register of licences?	Yes/No
If Yes, where is it kept?	
Licence information	
Application	
Type of licence	
Application	
Type of licence	
Application	
Type of licence	

9 Working healthily, safely and securely

Most people spend a considerable amount of time in their working environment. You need to be aware of potential hazards and the legislation that exists concerning health and safety. As the working environment changes and there is a greater use of new technology, you need to know about the particular health and safety factors involved.

There are two main aspects to consider: the general health and safety of the workplace, and factors specifically related to a technology-rich environment.

General health and safety

The main piece of legislation that relates to this is the Health and Safety at Work Act 1974. This legislation makes both the employer and the employee responsible for ensuring that the workplace is a safe and suitable place to work.

The employer must

- ensure that your workplace is safe and without risks to your health;
- ensure that the workplace is clean, and control the levels of dust, fumes and noise;
- ensure that both plant and machinery are safe to work with and that safe work practices are set and followed;
- provide you with all necessary information, instruction, training and supervision for your health and safety;
- put in place and implement a health and safety policy;
- provide any protective clothing and equipment that is specifically required by health and safety legislation;
- report injuries, diseases and dangerous incidents to the appropriate enforcing authority;
- provide adequate first aid facilities and training;
- take adequate precautions to prevent fire and provide appropriate means of fire fighting;
- provide adequate means of escape;
- maintain a workroom temperature of at least 16 °C after the first hour of work where employees do most of their work sitting down;
- provide, maintain and keep clean washing and toilet facilities;
- ensure that employees do not have to lift, carry or move any load so heavy that it is likely to injure them; and
- ensure that objects and substances are stored and used safely.

As an employee, you are required to be responsible for the health and safety of yourself and others and must co-operate with your employer, and

- follow the organisation's routine health and safety procedures and practices;
- take appropriate action if a hazardous or potentially hazardous situation arises; and
- ensure that your own work area is tidy and free from hazards.

Hazards in the working environment

Many aspects of the working environment present a hazard or potential hazard. Hazards are those aspects of the environment, the equipment and working practices which are unsafe. A potential hazard is often something less obvious.

When does a potential hazard become a hazard? This could result from

- carelessness or lack of attention;
- lack of foresight;
- rushing tasks or taking short-cuts;
- a coincidence of circumstances; or
- a change in circumstances.

Almost all hazards are avoidable if thought about beforehand.

Most workplaces have potential hazards which can result in accidents, such as the following:

- The shiny floor turns into a skating rink when a cup of coffee is spilt on it.
- The open window gets caught by a sudden strong gust of wind, slams shut and shatters.
- The fizzy drink beside the computer gets knocked over and not only damages the keyboard but also causes an electrical hazard.
- The filing cabinet drawer next to your desk is left open where someone could trip over it.
- The computer is moved to another part of the room and now there is a lot of stress on the cables as they only just reach.
- From the laser printer in the main working area, particles of toner are being continually released into the air.
- Passage ways are obstructed.
- Cables are frayed or damaged.
- Plugs are unearthed.

What should you do about a hazard? If it is within your control – deal with it:

- Make sure that when boxes of stationery are delivered they are put away safely.

- Move the waste bin from the passage way before someone trips up.
- Explain the dangers of using a swivel chair to stand on.

If it isn't within your control, report it to someone who can deal with it.

Figure 9.1 shows a picture of a typical modern office. However, it is not an entirely safe environment. Draw up two lists, one containing existing hazards and the other to include aspects that have the potential to be unsafe. Identify which of these would be within your authority to deal with and what you would do in each case. What procedures would you follow for those which were outside your authority? Include this information and a copy of the picture in your evidence folder.

Figure 9.1 A hazardous working environment

Can you recognise the commonly used safety symbols? In Figure 9.2, there are a number of standard health and safety signs and symbols. Complete the details of what they stand for. Locate examples of these in your workplace and note this down on the figure.

Sign	Indicates
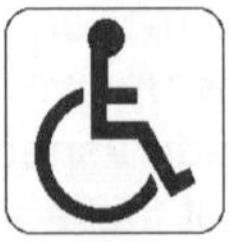 ♿	
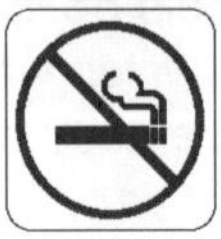 🚭	
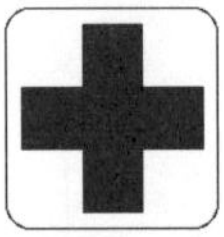 ✚	
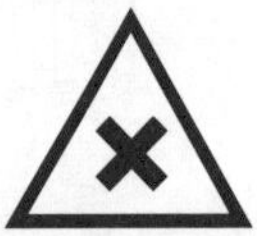 ⚠✕	
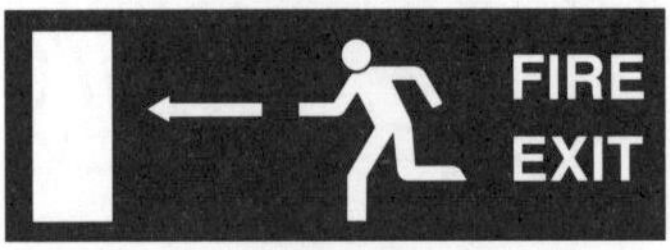 ← FIRE EXIT	
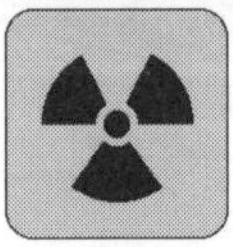 ☢	
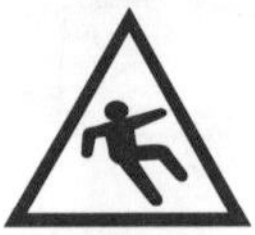 ⚠	
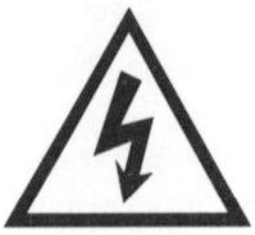 ⚠	

Figure 9.2 Health and safety signs and symbols

Emergencies

Accidents

Employers are required to take all reasonable steps to make sure that the workplace is a safe environment. Any accidents that do occur must be reported and recorded. This record has to be kept for 30 years. The circumstances of the accident must be investigated and, if it is serious, may have to be reported to the HSE (Health and Safety Executive).

CHECK IT YOURSELF

What is the procedure in your working environment for reporting and recording accidents? What information is recorded and who is responsible for maintaining these records? Enter this information in section 1 of health and safety checklist 1 given at the end of this chapter.

First aid

Under the Health and Safety (First Aid) Regulations, organisations are required to provide first aid facilities including qualified first aiders, first aid boxes and sometimes a first aid room. The level of provision is determined on the basis of the size of the organisation and how hazardous the environment is deemed to be. An office is potentially far less hazardous than a building site, for example. First aid boxes are not allowed to contain drugs nor can first aiders give out any medication – they could leave themselves open to legal action if someone had an adverse reaction to a drug he or she had been given.

CHECK IT YOURSELF

What first aid facilities are provided in your workplace? The names and contact numbers of all first aiders should be prominently displayed. Can you locate this information? What is kept in the first aid box nearest to your work area? Enter all this information in section 2 of health and safety checklist 1.

Illness

If you are ill at home, you will normally be required to notify your supervisor, line manager or tutor that you are unable to come to work. You would then possibly arrange to see your doctor. However, there are times when you or a colleague may become unwell whilst at work. In some instances, it may be necessary for a person who is unwell to go home. The person's supervisor should be notified, and assistance may be needed to get home.

In situations where an emergency arises, and you do not know the correct thing to do, make sure that you call a first aider immediately and don't try to deal with something outside your own scope. This can make things much worse.

Many organisations will welcome applications by staff to become first aiders and will provide the necessary training. The expertise and knowledge you get on a first aid course are extremely valuable, not just at work, so consider finding out about it.

Fire

Employers can take a number of precautions against fire. For example, they can

- install fire doors;
- install fire extinguishers;
- install smoke detectors and sprinkler systems;
- restrict or ban smoking; and
- arrange regular fire inspections with the fire brigade.

CHECK IT YOURSELF

If there were a fire, would you know what to do? Do you know the fire procedures in your workplace? If not, find out. Are details posted around the building? Who is responsible for ensuring that there are adequate notices and information for all occupants of the building? Write a brief report outlining all this and place it in your evidence folder.

For the purposes of fire-fighting, fires are grouped into a number of different types (see Figure 9.3). A range of different fire extinguishers are available to cater for all these categories (see Figure 9.4).

Class of fire	Substance burning
A	Paper, wood, fabric
B	Liquids, fat, paint, spirits, oil
C	Gases such as oxygen
D	Metals such as magnesium
Electrical	

Figure 9.3 Types of fires

Colour	Contents	Class of fire
Red	Water	A
Green	Halon, BCF	A,B,C, electrical
Cream	Foam	A,B,C
Chrome	Gas	A,B,C, electrical
Black	CO_2	B,C, electrical
Blue	Powder	D

Figure 9.4 Types of fire extinguishers

CHECK IT YOURSELF

In the area where you carry out most of your computer work, is there a fire extinguisher? What type is it? Is it appropriate for your area? Add this detail to your report on fire procedures.

Fire extinguishers should be checked on a regular basis to ensure they are ready for use when needed. This information should be displayed on each extinguisher.

CHECK IT YOURSELF

When was the fire extinguisher in your work area last checked? Find out who is responsible for this task. Has it ever been used? Add this information to your report. When the report is complete, give a copy to your supervisor, making sure it identifies any potential hazards or breaches of the legislation.

Evacuation

A number of circumstances, in addition to fire, may make it necessary to evacuate the building. These include

- bomb threats
- severe flooding
- gas leaks.

The organisation where you work should have regular fire/evacuation drills and the alarms should be tested frequently to ensure they all work.

When was the last evacuation drill you were involved in? Who is responsible for organising these? Enter this information in section 3 of health and safety checklist 1.

Factors specific to a technology-rich environment

There are still many uncertainties about aspects of a modern, technology-based working environment. Even now, not a great deal of information is available about the long-term effects of working in this kind of environment. Many people are understandably anxious about the possible effects, and in the past few years there has been a tightening up of the regulations and legal obligations of employers. The main legislation that relates to employers' obligations is primarily concerned with the use of display screen equipment (VDUs).

Health and Safety (Display Screen Equipment) Regulations 1992

The display screen equipment directives and the regulations contain very specific employer requirements in relation to employees working with display screen equipment. You should be aware that these regulations apply **only** to employees. However, they are based upon good, safe working practice and ideally should exist in *all* computer areas, at home, work or college.

Regulation 1: the user

The regulations define a user as an employee required to work at

- a workstation on the employer's premises;
- a workstation at home; or
- a workstation on another employer's premises.

The following factors are helpful in deciding if an employee is a user to which these regulations apply:

- The person relies on the use of display screen equipment to do the job.
- The person has no choice as to whether to use the equipment.
- Specific skills or training in the use of the equipment are necessary to do the job.
- The job can be carried out only through the use of the equipment for continuous spells of an hour or more at a time on a regular basis, probably daily.
- The job requires the fast transfer of information between the user and screen.

- The job demands high levels of attention and concentration by the user.

(**NOTE**: the definition of equipment excludes calculators, cash registers and typewriters with a small display screen.)

CHECK IT YOURSELF

Do you qualify as a *user*? Would you qualify, but for the fact that you are a student or trainee rather than an employee?

Regulation 2: risk analysis

This requires that the employer carries out a workstation assessment. The assessment must be a suitable and sufficient analysis to assess the health and safety risks the users may be exposed to as a result of using the equipment. It must include all workstations used by employees, regardless of who provided them.

The assessment should identify the risks in the *work space*:

- Is the workstation designed and positioned so that the user is able to change position?
- Is the room lighting satisfactory and does it provide adequate contrast?
- Are there reflections and glare?
- What levels of noise are emitted by the equipment?
- What levels of heat are generated by the equipment?
- Are there more than negligible levels of radiation, other than those in the visible part of the electromagnetic spectrum?
- Are adequate humidity levels established and maintained?

And *interfaces*:

- Is the software suitable for the task?
- Is the software easy to use and, where appropriate, can it be adapted to the level of knowledge or experience of the operator?
- Does the software provide feedback to the operator on performance of the systems?
- Does the software display information in a format and at a pace that can be adapted to meet the needs of the operator?

This assessment will often identify a number of areas for concern, and these will need further evaluation and corrective action to reduce the risks.

The codes of practice identify three general categories of risk to health:

Bad posture
- Most of these risks may be overcome by simple adjustments to ways of working.
- Will often highlight the need for training.

Damage to eyesight
- These risks may need only simple remedies such as repositioning of equipment or the use of blinds.
- Glare and reflections can be prevented by co-ordinating workplace and workstation artificial light.

Fatigue and stress
- These risks may be reduced by considering the design of workstations.
- Remedies will often involve considering rest periods or the pace of work.

Regulation 3: new workstations

From 1997 the employer must ensure that all workstations, not only those put into service since 1 January 1993, meet the requirements laid down in the schedules to the regulations.

Regulation 4: breaks

The employer is required to organise the activities of users so that their daily work using display screen equipment is regularly interrupted by breaks or changes of activity to reduce their continuous work at that equipment.

The codes of practice recommend that

- breaks should be taken *before* fatigue sets in and not to recuperate from it;
- frequent short breaks are preferable, e.g. 5–10 minutes every hour; and
- these breaks should be taken *away* from the display screen.

Jobs that involve a mixture of screen and non-screen work may well have sufficient breaks away from the screen to make scheduled breaks unnecessary.

Regulation 5: eyes and eyesight

If you are a regular, substantial user of display screen equipment or about to become one, you are entitled to ask for eye and eyesight tests. They must be carried out as soon as practicable by a competent person and usually before you become a user. Thereafter regular check-ups can be requested.

Where it is found that you need special corrective appliances (usually spectacles) the cost of these has to be borne by the employer. This does not cover persons who need normal eyesight correction, but only a special type required to deal specifically with a problem in using VDUs.

Regulation 6: provision of training

Where an employee is a user or is about to become a user, the employer must ensure that

- the employee is provided with adequate health and safety training in the use of any workstation upon which he or she may be required to work; and
- whenever there is any substantial modification to the workstation the user must be provided with adequate health and safety training.

Regulation 7: provision of information

The employer must ensure that

- all users are provided with adequate information about all aspects of health and safety relating to their workstation; and
- all users are informed of measures taken by the employer in compliance with duties under regulation 2 (assessment) and regulation 3 (workstations) as related to them and their work.

CHECK IT YOURSELF

Find out who is responsible in your working environment for ensuring that the organisation complies with health and safety regulations. If there are breaches of the regulations, to whom would you report them – your immediate supervisor, a health and safety rep, your tutor?

Good practice when working with VDUs

There are many examples of good practice which can reduce risks to your health. Many of these you can introduce yourself, whilst others will require the co-operation and support of your employer or colleagues.

Figure 9.5 shows correct posture when seated at your workstation and the positioning of the equipment in relation to you.

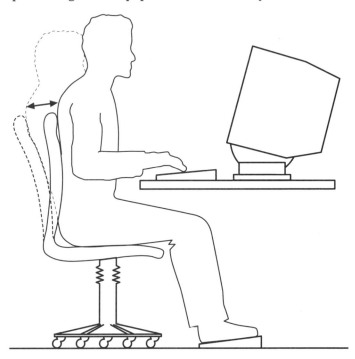

Figure 9.5   Correct posture for sitting at a workstation

One of the most important aspects of your workstation is that it should be adjustable to fit you or whoever is working there. When you get into the driving seat of a car you adjust the seating position for comfort and safe access to the controls. You should do the same when you sit down at your workstation.

Always check the following:

The height of your chair
- You should have sufficient space below the desk top to be able to move your legs freely.
- You may need a foot rest so that the back of your legs and knees do not have excess pressure on them.
- Your arms should be horizontal and your eyes should be on a level with the top of the VDU.

The support of your chair
- Your back should be supported but without undue pressure.

Mobility of your sitting position
- You should not sit in the same position for too long.
- You need to be able to move the position of your chair with ease in relation to the workstation and the different tasks you are likely to carry out.

The image on the screen
- Adjust the brightness and contrast so that they are comfortable for you – the image should be sharply focused and easy to read.
- Clean your screen regularly, as dirt and finger marks distort the image.
- Choose appropriate colour schemes where possible.

The layout of the workstation
- Move the keyboard, mouse mat, mouse and monitor to meet your work needs.
- Are you left or right handed? You can change your mouse installation to accommodate this.
- Make sure you don't need to bend your hands up at the wrists when using the keyboard.
- Make sure you have sufficient space for papers, disk boxes, etc. If you frequently work from paper documents a document holder may improve the comfort of your workstation. A cluttered workspace will make for reduced productivity as well as fatigue.

The lighting conditions in the room
- Bright lights should not reflect on the screen – you may need blinds to reduce sunlight at certain times of the day.
- The location of the workstation needs to take into account both natural and artificial lighting.
- Do you have sufficient light on the papers you are working from?

CHECK IT YOURSELF

How safe and suitable is your workstation? Complete the health and safety checklist 2 given at the end of this chapter to carry out an assessment. Speak to your supervisor about any problems you find and discuss what changes can be made.

RSI (repetitive strain injury)

This is a condition from which quite a number of people suffer. It is an extremely painful and sometimes quite debilitating injury. It is most likely to occur in people who are carrying out small, rapid movements of the hands, fingers and wrists. It would appear to be something that can be brought about by incorrect posture at the keyboard or excessive use without rest. Typists on old typewriters were less likely to get it because the range of movement required to operate a manual keyboard was much greater. Using a mouse, particularly for long periods of time without a break, can also be a cause.

The best thing for you to do, particularly if you use a keyboard or mouse for long periods at a time, is to make sure that

- you have set the keyboard so that it is most comfortable for you;
- you position your hands correctly over the keys; and
- you take suitable breaks.

Health and safety checklist 1

Section 1: accidents		
Is there a formal procedure for reporting accidents? If yes, place a copy in your evidence folder	Yes/No	
What information is recorded in the accident record book?	Details of the injured person	☐
	Details of the injury	☐
	Details of the accident	
	date	☐
	time	☐
	place	☐
	what happened	☐
	Treatment received	☐
	Name of witness (if any)	☐
Details of responsible person	Name	
	Job title	
Section 2: first aid		
What is the name of your nearest first aider? How can you contact him or her?		
What is kept in your nearest first aid box?	Individually wrapped sterile bandages	☐
	Sterile eye pads	☐
	Triangular bandages	☐
	Safety pins	☐
	Eye bath	☐
	Sterile water for eye baths	☐
	Sterile wound dressings in different sizes	☐
	Other	_____
Section 3: evacuation		
Name of responsible person		
Date and time of last evacuation drill you took part in		

Health and safety checklist 2: workstations

	Yes	No
Screen		
Is the screen large enough?		
Is the image stable and flicker-free?		
Can you adjust the image so that it is sharply focused?		
Can you adjust the colour scheme to suit your needs?		
Can you adjust the angle of the screen?		
Keyboard		
Is the keyboard of an appropriate size?		
Can you feel or hear the keys when pressed?		
Is there sufficient space to arrange it to suit your needs?		
Workstation		
Is your chair comfortable?		
Is the seat height and tilt adjustable?		
Is the height of the back-rest adjustable?		
Is the back-rest adjustable to fit your back?		
Does the chair swivel?		
Is the chair mobile?		
Have you been given information on adjusting your chair?		
Do you have sufficient leg room?		
Can you adjust the height of the desk top?		
Do you need a foot-rest?		
Is a foot-rest provided?		
Is a document holder available?		
Working environment		
Is there excessive glare in the work area?		
Are there reflections on your screen from the window?		
Are blinds fitted in the room?		
Are the lights too bright?		
Do you need more directed lighting?		
Is the desk top too shiny?		

Appendix: Applying for a job

There are a number of different ways to apply for a job. You might reply to an advertisement or could be making an enquiry on the recommendation of a friend. You might register with an employment agency who will try to find you a job or you might even try 'cold calling', that is approaching employers directly to see if they have any vacancies for which they might consider you.

Employers have different requirements when they are recruiting staff. Some will want you to write a letter of application, some will have an application form that you must complete and others will want you to give them a copy of your CV. Many will also want you to submit some sort of statement about why you are particularly suitable for the job.

The whole process of job applications can be quite stressful and time consuming. What you can do to reduce some of the pressure is to prepare outline documents with all the main details collated in a coherent form. All you will then need to do is update them, if necessary, and customise them for each specific job application.

What is a CV?

CV stands for curriculum vitae. It is the main document you can use to describe yourself to a prospective employer. It contains details about your personal background, your aspirations and ambitions, your work experience, your skills and knowledge, your education and other relevant activities.

Your CV is not something that you can create just once – it needs to be kept up to date. It therefore makes sense to set it up as a word processed document that you can amend whenever you need to. With the high level of word processing skills that you will have developed whilst working towards your qualification, you should be able to produce a very professional and well presented document. This will not only enable you to describe yourself but will also give you the opportunity to demonstrate your IT and presentation skills to any prospective employer.

The layout and content of your CV will need to be varied according to its purpose. You will usually find that you will need to amend its emphasis to meet the specific requirements of the job you are applying for. It will need to be different if it is submitted as the main document, together with a letter of application, rather than accompanying an application form. It is also useful to have an outline CV which just contains the basic facts – dates, addresses, etc. – so that you can refer to it when completing any forms.

CV layout

As with most business documents, the style and presentation of CVs have changed over the years. This has to some extent been influenced by the technology available to produce the final document.

You need to be mindful of the audience for whom your CV is written. As this is a document that you want to be read in full, it must not be too long. It needs to have a clear presentation and be organised so that the reader can quickly gain an impression of you, your knowledge, expertise and skills. It is usual to organise your CV into distinct sections, making it easy to find the required information. Your CV needs to include sections on personal details, work experience, relevant skills and knowledge, education and training, interests and hobbies, etc., and references. A section on your personal objectives could also be included, giving details of your aspirations and goals.

Personal details need to include:

- Name – if you have changed your name you might need to indicate this, particularly if some of your qualifications are in a different name or referees knew you by another name.
- Title – you might want to include this, especially if you wish to be addressed in a particular way, such as Ms rather than Mrs or Miss, or Dr, etc.
- Date of birth – many prospective employers will want this information.
- Address – obviously a prospective employer needs to have an address, and possibly also a telephone number and even an e-mail address, at which to contact you.

There may be additional basic information that you wish to include here such as National Insurance number, work permit details, etc.

CHECK IT YOURSELF

Complete section 1 of the CV information sheet given in this Appendix, with all your personal details.

Work experience is the section that provides details of each organisation for which you have worked, and it should be presented in chronological order. You should include the name and address of the organisation, the dates you were working there, the title of the job you held, a brief description of the post specifying its tasks and responsibilities, and the salary or wages you received. If you are looking for your first job it is particularly important to include any work experience placements you have been on, any holiday or weekend jobs and any voluntary work you might have done.

CHECK IT YOURSELF

Complete section 2 of the CV information sheet with details of your work experience to date.

Relevant skills and knowledge is the section where you can identify the skills and expertise you have that are particularly relevant to the type of work you are seeking. You need to emphasise the IT skills you have, specifying which packages you can use and indicating some of the ways in which you have used them.

CHECK IT YOURSELF

Complete section 3 of the CV information sheet with details of the skills and knowledge you have that would be of interest to a prospective employer.

Education and training details need to include information about your education from age 11. This should include each school, college or other organisation you attended in chronological order. You need to give the name and address of the institution, the dates you attended, the subjects studied and qualifications gained. If you attended part time, you should also indicate this. As well as formal education, you should include any training courses you have attended which are particularly relevant to the type of work you are seeking, or which may increase your employability, for example a first aid certificate.

CHECK IT YOURSELF

Complete section 4 of the CV information sheet with details of your education to date and any training courses you have attended.

Interests and hobbies. Most employers are interested to know a little about their prospective employees in terms of what they do outside work. This is where your personality can come across in your CV. Prospective employers will be particularly interested in any activities that show leadership skills (for example, leading Scout or Guide activities), teamwork (such as sports teams, or ones that involve accepting responsibilities, such as acting as treasurer for a club or society.

Complete section 5 of the CV information sheet with information about your interests, hobbies and activities outside work.

References. Prospective employers will usually want to contact at least two people who can confirm your suitability for employment. They will want to know the name and relationship to you (e.g. manager, tutor) of people who can provide information about your attitude to work, your enthusiasm, commitment and skills. They will want to know that you are a reliable, honest and punctual worker. They will also need to be able to confirm your experience, qualifications and knowledge. For some jobs they will be particularly interested in confirming aspects that relate specifically to the type of job. For example, if the job involves working with the public, they will be interested in your ability to work with and relate to people, or if you are going to be handling money they will wish to ensure that you are trustworthy. Remember to ask permission from anyone you wish to use as a referee *before* giving details to a prospective employer.

CHECK IT YOURSELF

Complete section 6 of the CV information sheet with details of people you could ask to act as your referees.

You should also include a **personal objectives** section in your CV, in which you can show that this is the area of work or job for you. You will need to include a statement about how you wish your career to develop, and ensure that this relates to the opportunities in the job you are applying for.

What are your job/career plans? What sort of job are you looking for now, and what sort of work would you like to be doing in five years' time? Write a few clear sentences about both your short and long-term goals. Make sure they are realistic and that they make use of the skills, experience and knowledge gained in this NVQ. At this stage, if you are not applying for a particular job, this will probably be a fairly general statement, but remember that it will need to be revised each time you use it to reflect the particular job application.

It is important to make sure that your CV accounts for all the time from your secondary education onwards. If you had some time out after school before going to college or embarking on your career, indicate this; what were you doing? Travelling, gaining skills, doing voluntary work? If you have had time out as a parent, include this information.

CV information sheet

Section 1: personal details	
Name – including title	
Date of birth	
Address	
Telephone number, e-mail address, etc.	
NI number, etc.	
Section 2: work experience	
Employer (1) details	
Start and end date	
Job title	
Salary	
Description	
Employer (2) details	
Start and end date	
Job title	
Salary	
Description	
Employer (3) details	
Start and end date	
Job title	
Salary	
Description	

CV information sheet (continued)

Section 3: relevant skills and knowledge

Section 4: education and training

School (from age 11) name
and address

Start and end dates

Qualifications

College name and address

Start and end dates

Qualifications

Other courses attended

Section 5: interests and hobbies

Section 6: references

Referees – name, job title
and address
(1)

(2)

Application forms

The questions in application forms can vary quite considerably. Many organisations will require you to complete a form. In addition they may specifically state that you should *not* include a CV, or that a CV may be included but the form must still be completed in full. Much of the form will ask for basic details about yourself, your previous work experience and education and the qualifications you have gained. If you have prepared an outline CV, most of this is simply a matter of transferring the information to the form. There will also be a section (often little more than a blank page) where you are asked to write about why and how you are particularly suitable for the job. This is almost always the most important part of the form, and this is where you need to concentrate your efforts. In this section you should include information from your CV such as personal objectives, skills and knowledge, and relevant experience.

Make sure that you first read any guidance about how the form is to be completed. It may specify that the form must be filled in with black ink – this is usually to ensure that good-quality photocopies can be made – or it may even require that it is hand written. Some employers engage specialists to analyse your handwriting!

Letter of application

A letter of application will usually be used where there is no application form. Its purpose is to introduce your CV and to make clear which job you are applying for. You need to state clearly where you heard about the jobs and then highlight the particular skills and experience you have that make you suitable for the position. It is often appropriate to identify some recent training or work experience which is particularly relevant. You should also include details about your availability for interview and when you would be able to start work, should a post be offered to you. Don't make the letter more than one page long – it needs to be clear, brief and very much to the point.

When making an application in this way, you will need to ensure that your CV is comprehensive and supplies sufficient detail about yourself and why you should be considered for the job in question.

Which jobs should I apply for?

When looking at job advertisements, how do you decide which ones to apply for? You need to read the advertisements very carefully and identify ones that match your

- skills
- qualifications
- previous experience.

Suitable jobs should give you opportunities to

- achieve some of your goals
- extend your skills and knowledge
- increase your range of experience.

CHECK IT YOURSELF

On the next page are some examples of job advertisements. Choose one of the jobs and create a CV which you could use to apply for this job. Also write a letter of application to send with your CV. Examples of a letter of application and CV are included at the end of this Appendix.

Experienced Secretary/Audio Typist

Salary £14,000 pa

Required for small, busy firm of
Chartered Accountants

- Excellent Word6/7 skills
- Eye for detail
- Professional telephone manner
- Initiative
- Knowledge of Lotus/Excel advantage

Please send CV and covering letter to:

The Office Manager, Smythe and Parkes
Elm House, 27 Uxbridge Road
Oxford OX4 8AB

IT TRAINING

We are a large, lively firm of solicitors. We are looking for a bright and enthusiastic person to join our IT team to cross-train users from WordPerfect to Word 6. Further training needs may include Lotus Notes and other Windows applications.

Candidates should have a thorough knowledge of Word and other computer applications with some experience of training and an understanding of secretarial work.

This is a challenging post which offers an attractive salary package and opportunity for development to the right applicant.

Please send your cv to:
Mrs S Laundy, Candry and Singh, 30 Westminster Road, Coventry CV6 9LS

PR secretary   **to £18K**

Superb opportunity to join a leading PR Consultancy who promote prestigious clients in the scientific/medical industry.

Aside from the usual secretarial duties, you will organise press releases and monitoring, maintain a database and assist with desk

research. Good knowledge of Windows packages needed – Word, Access, Powerpoint, Internet and e-mail used. A minimum of two years' secretarial experienced required.

FLIGHTY
RECRUITMENT tel 0123 456 7890
Stafford House Potteries Road Bath BA3 6AE

OFFICE ADMINISTRATOR
Borehamwood
£7.20 p.h.

Experienced Office Administrator required to manage a busy Youth Service office. Enthusiastic person with ability to work on own and carry out office tasks is needed to complete the team.

Essential: Word processing, organised
Desirable: Spreadsheet and e-mail

Send your CV and letter of application to: Michelle Walters, Head of Youth Services Team, Council Offices, Borehamwood, Herts

---

PHARMACY DEPARTMENT–NHS TRUST HOSPITAL

Departmental Secretary – £9396–£10,910 pa

Applications are invited for the above post to work in the Pharmacy Department for inpatients and outpatients. The post requires working in the main for the principal pharmacist and her team. Team working is practised in the department and the post holder will be expected to organise the administrative functions of the department from filing to organising meetings.

- Ability to operate computer packages such as Windows, Word and Excel essential
- Proven organisational skills
- High level of accuracy
- Ability to work as part of a team.

Send letter of application and CV in the first instance to: Personnel Department, Jorvik Hospital, Minster Road, York YO8 2BD

Personnel Manager
Crink, Totem & Partners
Lancaster Road
Hull
LM3 4TQ

15 June 199X

Dear Ms Foulger

Office Administrator

I am writing in response to the advertisement for the above post in the local newspaper last Friday. Enclosed is my CV, which includes the details of two referees whom you may contact to confirm my suitability for the post.

I am presently completing a course at the local college in the use of a wide range of IT office applications, including word processing, spreadsheets, databases and the use of electronic communication systems. When I complete the course at the beginning of July I will have gained an NVQ Level 2 award in Using Information Technology. I am keen to return to full-time work as soon as the course is completed.

I have recently been working on a voluntary basis for a national charity, in their offices in the centre of town. During this time I have gained considerable experience in the application of the skills acquired in my studies. I am an extremely conscientious and enthusiastic person and like to work with others as part of a team.

I have also enclosed a stamped, addressed envelope for your reply.

Looking forward to hearing from you.

Yours sincerely

Curriculum Vitae

Personal details

Name: Christiane Baker

Date of birth: 15 June 1972

Address: 12a Wiley Street
Birmingham

Telephone: 01234 567 8901
E-mail: chris@abc.def.uk

NI Number: HT 12 34 56 G

Personal objectives
I have recently updated my IT skills and would now like to have the opportunity to use them in an office environment, while also using the interpersonal skills I have acquired through working in the hotel industry. I enjoy assisting others in the use of technology and would be interested in working in a job where I also had a user support and training role.

Work experience
Waverley Hotel Oct 1989–May 1993 **Receptionist**
Duties included receiving and registering guests, dealing with booking enquiries, making up guests' bills and some associated general clerical tasks.

Wiley Play Group **January 1995 onwards Volunteer helper**
Help with range of activities for children indoors and outside. I assist with the general clerical activities including word processing letters for parents and producing information leaflets and posters.

Relevant skills and knowledge
I have good general IT skills and have recent experience using the following packages:

word processing: Word 6 & 7
WordPerfect 6
spreadsheet: Excel 5
presentation: Powerpoint 4

Education and training
Hillside School Sept 1983–July 1989 5 GCSEs including Maths and English
Typewriting Stage 1

FE College Sept 1995–July 1996 Computer Literacy Certificate
(evening class)

FE College Jan 1997–June 1997 NVQ Level 2 Using IT
(full time)

Interests and hobbies
I am a keen gardener and also enjoy rock climbing.

Assessors   persons responsible within the NVQ centre for checking the quality of the evidence (work) produced by the candidates and making sure that it covers all the requirements of the standards.

Awarding body   the organisation, approved by the QCA, which awards the qualification, e.g. RSA Examinations Board.

Competence   ability to carry out the activities specified by the performance criteria to a particular standard.

Element   each unit consists of a number of elements - candidates need to demonstrate competence in all elements of a unit to be awarded the unit.

Evidence   the products, statements and other records that demonstrate competence - organised into a portfolio and assessed against the standards.

External verifier   person appointed by the awarding body to ensure that the NVQ centre is carrying out the assessment to the required national standards.

Internal verifier   the person within the NVQ centre with responsibility for ensuring that all the assessment in the centre is consistent and is being carried out to national standards - the link person with the awarding body's external verifier.

ITITO   Information Technology Industry Training Organisation - the computer industry lead body which sets the occupational standards.

NVQ   National Vocational Qualification - a standard that has been introduced throughout the country specifically for work-based qualifications.

Performance criteria   the things a candidate must be able to do satisfactorily in order to be able to claim the award.

QCA   Qualifications and Curriculum Authority - the organisation that oversees the standards and approves the qualifications set by the awarding bodies.

Range statements   set out the situations and conditions in which candidates must be able to work and the equipment they must be able to use.

Standards   the set of units defined by the industry lead body that describes the knowledge, skills and level of competence required for the area of work.

Underpinning knowledge   the knowledge necessary to be able to carry out the work-based activities.

Unit   all NVQs consist of a number of units - a unit is a complete section of knowledge and is the smallest award possible - most NVQs consist of a number of mandatory units and some optional units.

Alternate (ALT) key a key, similar to the *control* key, that is used together with another key to send a modified code to the computer.

Archive an archive copy of a file is made when you no longer need the file in the main working environment but need to keep a copy for reference or possible use in the future.

Backup an operating utility which lets you make a security copy of your files – this is not a directly usable copy but can be *restored* if required.

Bitmap graphics *images* created in pixels, i.e.consisting of blocks of colour.

Byte the unit of measurement for counting the size of various parts of a computer – generally speaking the computer space necessary to hold one character or code.

CD optical disk which is capable of holding high volumes of *data* – it can be created only once and is therefore not appropriate for data that needs to be changed.

CD-ROM compact disk – read-only memory drive.

Cell references the system by which an item or group of items of data in a *spreadsheet* are referenced, e.g. A4 (column A row 4).

Clip art collections of popular *images* and useful *graphics* that are made available to enhance the presentation of *documents*.

Control (CTRL) key a key that is used together with another key to modify the code sent to the computer.

Copy an operating utility command which lets you make a copy of a file on to another *disk* or into another *subdirectory* or into the same subdirectory but with a different *filename*.

Data the raw facts input into the computer.

Database an organised, structured collection of related *data* that is defined and processed using a database management system.

Data integrity this refers to ensuring the correctness of the *data* at all stages – at point of entry, throughout processing and at output.

Data Protection Act the legislation that exists to ensure the security and integrity of personal computer-based *data*.

Data security this is concerned with ensuring that *data* held on a computer system can be accessed or updated only by those users who have authority.

Default   the settings that the *hardware* and *software* are set to start up with.

Delete   an operating utility command which lets you erase a file.

Desktop publishing   software which enables the creation of artwork *documents* for publishing through the manipulation of text and *images*. Many *word processing* packages include DTP features, whilst 'high end' DTP will produce copy ready for final printing.

Diagnostic software   *software* designed to assist with fault finding.

Digitiser   an input device used for converting *data* in its current form into digital data which can be processed by the computer.

Directory   the information about the files stored on each *disk* to enable both the user and the computer *operating system* to locate the files on the disk – the directory will include details of the name, date and time created or updated, the location on the disk and the size of the file.

Disk   data storage medium – see *hard disk, floppy disk, CD-ROM*.

Disk drive   the mechanical device that drives the *disk* and operates the read/write heads to access the data – referenced by a letter followed by a colon, e.g. C:/

Document   term frequently used within a *word processing* package for a file which contains principally text and sometimes graphs and other *images*.

Electronic mail   known as e-mail – a communication system that enables messages and information to be sent electronically to other users – it is a way of carrying out rapid, text-based communication across an organisation and, potentially, outside it.

Environment   this is a 'user-friendly' way of working with the computer which hides the 'raw' *operating system* and lets the user carry out many of the basic functions through the use of *WIMPs*.

Escape (Esc) key   this key is used to send a command to the computer – different packages use this key in different ways but most frequently to cancel an instruction.

Extension   the second part of a *filename* in MS-DOS and some other *operating systems* – often used to indicate the type of file.

Fax (facsimile)   the transmission of exact copies of a document across the telephone network – any documents, whether hand-written or containing pictures, diagrams, graphs, charts or typed text can be transmitted at great speed for relatively low costs.

Filename every file has a name to identify and access it – the name must be unique within the *subdirectory* and *disk* that it is stored on – each *operating system* has a set of rules about the structure of filenames and permitted characters.

Floppy disk a lower capacity *disk,* usually 1.44 Mb, which is not kept permanently inside the computer but is removed when not being used.

Folder this is an alternative term used in some systems for *subdirectory.*

Footer the area below the main part of a page used to include text that can appear at the bottom of every page of the *document* and may include page numbers.

Format (noun) the way an item of *data* or a piece of text is presented.

Format (verb) the process of preparing a new unused *disk* for use with a particular *operating system* and *disk drive.*

Function keys there are usually twelve of these keys across the top of the *keyboard* and they are often set up to carry out commands for a particular package.

Gigabyte 1073741824 *bytes* – often referred to as one thousand million or an American billion.

Graphics there are two types – *vector* and *bitmap* images.

Graphics tablet a flat board connected to the computer on which you can draw *images* with a special pen – these are displayed directly on the *VDU* and can be stored in the computer.

Greyscale the digital progression of density in a monochrome image.

Hard disk a high-capacity *disk* which is usually permanently inside the computer.

Hard return the code included in a *word processing* document to indicate the end of a *paragraph,* achieved by pressing the return (also called enter) key.

Hardware the physical parts of the computer system.

Header the area above the main part of a page used to include text that can appear at the top of every page of the *document* and may include page numbers.

Housekeeping the management and maintenance of the *disk* filing system.

Icon an *image* which is used to represent a command or function you wish to carry out.

Image see *graphics*.

Index an alphabetical list usually with section and page references – the creation of this list is often a facility available in *word processing* packages based on marked text.

Information processed *data* that has been given meaning – the output from the computer.

Ink-jet printer output device used to produce good-quality printouts – particularly cost-effective for colour printouts.

Internet an international network of computers that makes possible the worldwide interchange of *information* – can be accessed through an Internet provider.

IT information technology – a term used generally to describe the use of computers to capture, process and provide *information*.

Keyboard one of the main input devices and frequently including the standard QWERTY keys, a numeric keypad, cursor control keys and *function keys* – this type of keyboard is known as an extended or 102-key keyboard.

Kilobyte 1024 *bytes* – often referred to as one thousand bytes.

Landscape the *orientation* of the printed *document* so that the paper is wider than it is long.

Laser printer output device used to produce high-quality printouts.

Licence an authority to use a piece of *software* – most software is supplied under some form of licence.

Light pen a pen-shaped input device which is pointed at the *screen* to make selections or to create *images*.

Megabyte 1048576 *bytes* – often referred to as one million bytes.

Memory temporary storage areas.

Menu a set of options (drop down or pull down) which is usually used to give you a choice from a number of similar commands or functions.

Monitor see *VDU*.

Mouse this is an input device with one, two or three buttons, with a ball underneath which is moved across a flat surface to control a *pointer* on the screen.

Network a number of computers and peripherals connected together in order to share resources and give access to *data*, and to provide communication facilities between users.

Newspaper columns   in *word processing* this refers to columns of text that flow from top to bottom and continue at the top.

Numeric keypad   usually on the right-hand side of the keyboard with numbers 0–9 and the four calculation symbols (+-*/) and an enter key – mainly used for rapid input of numeric *data*.

Numerical models   a defined set of rules to calculate or project numerical *data* – *spreadsheet software* is one of the most frequently used *packages* to achieve this.

Object   a discrete item contained within a *word processing* document, e.g. an imported *image*.

Operating system   the sets of instructions and rules that enable the different parts of the computer to work together – it will include *software* to start the computer, to interpret each key pressed and display it on the *screen*, to save the work you do and to communicate with any devices attached to the system, such as *disk drives*, *printers*, *plotters* or devices to communicate with other computers.

Orientation   the direction of the printed *document* – see *landscape* and *portrait*.

Package   a set of programs that can be bought 'off-the-shelf' to meet the needs of a particular application.

Paragraph   in *word processing* a paragraph is all the text between two *hard returns* – many *formatting* functions and particularly word wrap and justification are applied a paragraph at a time.

Parallel columns   in *word processing* this refers to columns of text where each block of text in a column starts on the same line as that in the column adjacent to it.

Password   a secret code entered by the user to gain access to the computer or to an area of the *data* and systems; used to maintain *data security*.

Path   the way to a file on a *disk* – this path indicates the route from the *directory* you are currently working in, within the directory tree, to the *subdirectory* where the file is located.

Plotter   an output device used to produce high-quality *graphics* data – the *image* is created using a number of different-coloured pens picked up and put down by an 'arm' that moves across the paper.

Pointer   used to select an option or position on the *screen* – this pointer will usually be controlled through the use of an input device such as a *mouse* or *light pen*.

Portrait   the *orientation* of the printed *document* so that the paper is longer than it is wide.

Printer   an output device used to produce a permanent paper-based copy – sometimes referred to as hard copy – see *laser printer* and *ink-jet printer*.

Processor   the part of the computer that carries out the instructions.

RAM   random access memory – the part of *memory* which temporarily holds the programs (instructions) you are using and the *data* you are inputting – it is usually volatile, that is, when you switch off the computer anything in RAM that has not been stored will be lost.

Restore   an operating utility which lets you recreate a usable copy of your files from a *backup* copy.

ROM   (read-only memory) – this is a part of *memory* that you can read from only, you cannot change it by adding, editing or deleting anything.

Root directory   this is the main *directory* set up on each *disk* when it is *formatted* – it is referenced by the use of the back slash (\).

Scanner   an input device used to capture *images* and text from the printed page.

Screen   see *VDU*.

Setup   the way the system, *software* and *hardware*, has been installed and organised to enable the user to get the best from it in terms of *memory*, type of printing facilities and most frequently used aspects of the *packages*.

Soft return   the start of a new line inserted by the *software* to meet the *paragraph* margins – it is automatically adjusted as necessary to take into account any changes to the content or layout of the paragraph.

Software   programs or sets of instructions to carry out a computer operation or application.

Sound card   a circuit board which enables high-quality sound to be produced on the computer – essential when using multimedia *software*.

Spellcheck   a facility available in many packages including *word processing*, *spreadsheets* and *desktop publishing* to check the spelling and to offer possible corrections from a dictionary – dictionaries are often available for a number of languages.

Spreadsheet   a generic package which provides a freeform tool for calculations and the creation of numerical models.

Subdirectory   a subdivision of a *directory* – the system is hierarchical and enables you to organise files so that you can find them more easily.

Systems software   the *software* that enables the computer to work.

Table of contents   this lists the main headings and subheadings for each section of a *document* – this list is in sequential order and will usually include page numbers – the creation of such a table of contents is often a facility available in *word processing* packages based on marked text.

VDU   visual display unit – the output device which enables the computer to communicate with you; both what you input and the responses from the system appear on this device – may also be referred to as a monitor or screen.

Vector graphics   images constructed using lines with precise start and end points – typically used for technical applications, as the resulting images are more precise and better able to be manipulated as *objects*.

Virus   piece of *software* which can attach itself to a storage area (*disk* or *memory*) and cause errors to occur in the operation of the computer or damage to the *data*.

WIMPs   stands for *Windows, Icons, Menus* and *Pointers*.

Window   an area of a screen which lets you view an activity – you can have more than one window open at any time and can therefore look at and work on a number of different activities at the same time.

Word processing   *software* which enables the creation, saving, editing and printing of *documents* – modern word processing facilities include not only sophisticated text manipulation and presentation functions but the facility for integration of *data* from other *packages* and the inclusion of graphical *images*.

Workstation   the complete work space of the user – this includes not only the main parts of the computer but also the mouse mat, desk, chair, lighting, etc.

Index